CHRISTINA GEORGINA ROSSETTI (5 December 1830– 29 December 1894) was an English writer of romantic, devotional and children's poems, including "Goblin Market" and "Remember". She also wrote the words of two Christmas carols well known in Britain: "In the Bleak Midwinter", later set by Gustav Holst, Katherine Kennicott Davis, and Harold Darke, and "Love Came Down at Christmas", also set by Darke and other composers. She was a sister of the artist and poet Dante Gabriel Rossetti II and features in several of his paintings.

Christina Rossetti

100 SELECTED POEMS

DELHI OPEN BOOKS

100 SELECTED POEMS
BY CHRISTINA ROSSETTI

Published by

Delhi Open Books
G/F, 4771/23, Bharat Ram Road, Daryaganj, New Delhi-110002
Ph.: 91-11-42408081
E-mail: delhiopenbooks2016@gmail.com

ISBN: 978-93-94109-71-1

Cover, Typesetting, and Book Design by ROHIT

Printed & bound in India

Contents

A Baby's Cradle With No Baby In It

A baby's cradle with no baby in it,
A baby's grave where autumn leaves drop sere;
The sweet soul gathered home to Paradise,
The body waiting here.

A Ballad Of Boding

There are sleeping dreams and waking dreams;
What seems is not always as it seems.
I looked out of my window in the sweet new morning,
And there I saw three barges of manifold adorning
Went sailing toward the East:
The first had sails like fire,
The next like glittering wire,
But sackcloth were the sails of the least;
And all the crews made music, and two had spread a feast.
The first choir breathed in flutes,
And fingered soft guitars;
The second won from lutes
Harmonious chords and jars,
With drums for stormy bars:
But the third was all of harpers and scarlet trumpeters;
Notes of triumph, then
An alarm again,
As for onset, as for victory, rallies, stirs,
Peace at last and glory to the vanquishers.
The first barge showed for figurehead a Love with wings;
The second showed for figurehead a Worm with stings;
The third, a Lily tangled to a Rose which clings.
The first bore for freight gold and spice and down;
The second bore a sword, a sceptre, and a crown;
The third, a heap of earth gone to dust and brown.
Winged Love meseemed like Folly in the face;
Stinged Worm meseemed loathly in his place;
Lily and Rose were flowers of grace.
Merry went the revel of the fire-sailed crew,
Singing, feasting, dancing to and fro:
Pleasures ever changing, ever graceful, ever new;
Sighs, but scarce of woe;

All the sighing
Wooed such sweet replying;
All the sighing, sweet and low,

Used to come and go
For more pleasure, merely so.
Yet at intervals some one grew tired
Of everything desired,
And sank, I knew not whither, in sorry plight,
Out of sight.
The second crew seemed ever
Wider-visioned, graver,
More distinct of purpose, more sustained of will;
With heads erect and proud,
And voices sometimes loud;
With endless tacking, counter-tacking,
All things grasping, all things lacking,
It would seem;
Ever shifting helm, or sail, or shroud,
Drifting on as in a dream.
Hoarding to their utmost bent,
Feasting to their fill,
Yet gnawed by discontent,
Envy, hatred, malice, on their road they went.
Their freight was not a treasure,
Their music not a pleasure;
The sword flashed, cleaving through their bands,
Sceptre and crown changed hands.
The third crew as they went
Seemed mostly different;
They toiled in rowing, for to them the
wind was contrary,
As all the world might see.
They labored at the oar,
While on their heads they bore
The fiery stress of sunshine more and more.
They labored at the oar hand-sore,

Till rain went splashing,
And spray went dashing,
Down on them, and up on them, more and more.
Their sails were patched and rent,
Their masts were bent,
In peril of their lives they worked and went.
For them no feast was spread,
No soft luxurious bed

Scented and white,
No crown or sceptre hung in sight;
In weariness and painfulness,
In thirst and sore distress,
They rowed and steered from left to right
With all their might.
Their trumpeters and harpers round about
Incessantly played out,
And sometimes they made answer with a shout;
But oftener they groaned or wept,
And seldom paused to eat, and seldom slept.
I wept for pity watching them, but more
I wept heart-sore
Once and again to see
Some weary man plunge overboard, and swim
To Love or Worm ship floating buoyantly:
And there all welcomed him.
The ships steered each apart and seemed to scorn each other,
Yet all the crews were interchangeable;
Now one man, now another,
—Like bloodless spectres some, some flushed by health,—
Changed openly, or changed by stealth,
Scaling a slippery side, and scaled it well.
The most left Love ship, hauling wealth
Up Worm ship's side;
While some few hollow-eyed
Left either for the sack-sailed boat;
But this, though not remote,

Was worst to mount, and whoso left it once
Scarce ever came again,
But seemed to loathe his erst companions,
And wish and work them bane.
Then I knew (I know not how) there lurked quicksands full of dread,
Rocks and reefs and whirlpools in the water-bed,
Whence a waterspout
Instantaneously leaped out,
Roaring as it reared its head.
Soon I spied a something dim,
Many-handed, grim,

That went flitting to and fro the first and second ship;
It puffed their sails full out
With puffs of smoky breath
From a smouldering lip,
And cleared the waterspout
Which reeled roaring round about
Threatening death.
With a horny hand it steered,
And a horn appeared
On its sneering head upreared
Haughty and high
Against the blackening lowering sky.
With a hoof it swayed the waves;
They opened here and there,
Till I spied deep ocean graves
Full of skeletons
That were men and women once
Foul or fair;
Full of things that creep
And fester in the deep
And never breathe the clean life-nurturing air.
The third bark held aloof
From the Monster with the hoof,
Despite his urgent beck,
And fraught with guile

Abominable his smile;
Till I saw him take a flying leap on to that deck.
Then full of awe,
With these same eyes I saw
His head incredible retract its horn
Rounding like babe's new born,
While silvery phosphorescence played
About his dis-horned head.
The sneer smoothed from his lip,
He beamed blandly on the ship;
All winds sank to a moan,
All waves to a monotone
(For all these seemed his realm),
While he laid a strong caressing hand upon the helm.
Then a cry well nigh of despair

Shrieked to heaven, a clamor of desperate prayer.
The harpers harped no more,
While the trumpeters sounded sore
An alarm to wake the dead from their bed:
To the rescue, to the rescue, now or never,
To the rescue, O ye living, O ye dead,
Or no more help or hope for ever!—
The planks strained as though they must part asunder,
The masts bent as though they must dip under,
And the winds and the waves at length
Girt up their strength,
And the depths were laid bare,
And heaven flashed fire and volleyed thunder
Through the rain-choked air,
And sea and sky seemed to kiss
In the horror and the hiss
Of the whole world shuddering everywhere.
Lo! a Flyer swooping down
With wings to span the globe,
And splendor for his robe
And splendor for his crown.

He lighted on the helm with a foot of fire,
And spun the Monster overboard:
And that monstrous thing abhorred,
Gnashing with balked desire,
Wriggled like a worm infirm
Up the Worm
Of the loathly figurehead.
There he crouched and gnashed;
And his head re-horned, and gashed
From the other's grapple, dripped bloody red.
I saw that thing accurst
Wreak his worst
On the first and second crew:
Some with baited hook
He angled for and took,
Some dragged overboard in a net he threw,
Some he did to death
With hoof or horn or blasting breath.

I heard a voice of wailing
Where the ships went sailing,
A sorrowful voice prevailing
Above the sound of the sea,
Above the singers' voices,
And musical merry noises;
All songs had turned to sighing,
The light was failing,
The day was dying—
Ah me,
That such a sorrow should be!
There was sorrow on the sea and sorrow on the land
When Love ship went down by the bottomless quicksand
To its grave in the bitter wave.
There was sorrow on the sea and sorrow on the land
When Worm ship went to pieces on the rock-bound strand,
And the bitter wave was its grave.
But land and sea waxed hoary

In whiteness of a glory
Never told in story
Nor seen by mortal eye,
When the third ship crossed the bar
Where whirls and breakers are,
And steered into the splendors of the sky;
That third bark and that least
Which had never seemed to feast,
Yet kept high festival above sun and moon and star.

A Better Ressurection

I have no wit, no words, no tears;
My heart within me like a stone
Is numbed too much for hopes or fears.
Look right, look left, I dwell alone;
I lift mine eyes, but dimmed with grief
No everlasting hills I see;
My life is in the falling leaf:
O Jesus, quicken me.
My life is like a faded leaf,
My harvest dwindled to a husk:
Truly my life is void and brief
And tedious in the barren dusk;
My life is like a frozen thing,
No bud nor greenness can I see:
Yet rise it shall--the sap of spring;
O Jesus, rise in me.
My life is like a broken bowl,
A broken bowl that cannot hold
One drop of water for my soul
Or cordial in the searching cold;
Cast in the fire the perished thing;
Melt and remould it, till it be
A royal cup for Him, my King:
O Jesus, drink of me.

A Bird's-Eye View

'Croak, croak, croak,'
Thus the Raven spoke,
Perched on his crooked tree
As hoarse as hoarse could be.
Shun him and fear him,
Lest the Bridegroom hear him;
Scout him and rout him
With his ominous eye about him.
Yet, 'Croak, croak, croak,'
Still tolled from the oak;
From that fatal black bird,
Whether heard or unheard:
'O ship upon the high seas,
Freighted with lives and spices,
Sink, O ship,' croaked the Raven:
'Let the Bride mount to heaven.'
In a far foreign land,
Upon the wave-edged sand,
Some friends gaze wistfully
Across the glittering sea.
'If we could clasp our sister,'
Three say, 'now we have missed her!'
'If we could kiss our daughter!'
Two sigh across the water.
Oh, the ship sails fast
With silken flags at the mast,
And the home-wind blows soft;
But a Raven sits aloft,
Chuckling and choking,
Croaking, croaking, croaking:—
Let the beacon-fire blaze higher;
Bridegroom, watch; the Bride draws nigher.
On a sloped sandy beach,

Which the spring-tide billows reach,
Stand a watchful throng

Who have hoped and waited long:
'Fie on this ship, that tarries
With the priceless freight it carries.
The time seems long and longer:
O languid wind, wax stronger;'—
Whilst the Raven perched at ease
Still croaks and does not cease,
One monotonous note
Tolled from his iron throat:
'No father, no mother,
But I have a sable brother:
He sees where ocean flows to,
And he knows what he knows, too.'
A day and a night
They kept watch worn and white;
A night and a day
For the swift ship on its way:
For the Bride and her maidens
—Clear chimes the bridal cadence—
For the tall ship that never
Hove in sight for ever.
On either shore, some
Stand in grief loud or dumb
As the dreadful dread
Grows certain though unsaid.
For laughter there is weeping,
And waking instead of sleeping,
And a desperate sorrow
Morrow after morrow.
Oh, who knows the truth,
How she perished in her youth,
And like a queen went down
Pale in her royal crown:
How she went up to glory

From the sea-foam chill and hoary,
From the sea-depth black and riven
To the calm that is in Heaven?

They went down, all the crew,
The silks and spices too,
The great ones and the small,
One and all, one and all.
Was it through stress of weather,
Quicksands, rocks, or all together?
Only the Raven knows this,
And he will not disclose this.—
After a day and year
The bridal bells chime clear;
After a year and a day
The Bridegroom is brave and gay:
Love is sound, faith is rotten;
The old Bride is forgotten:—
Two ominous Ravens only
Remember, black and lonely.

A Birthday

My heart is like a singing bird
Whose nest is in a water'd shoot;
My heart is like an apple-tree
Whose boughs are bent with thickset fruit;
My heart is like a rainbow shell
That paddles in a halcyon sea;
My heart is gladder than all these
Because my love is come to me.
Raise me a dais of silk and down;
Hang it with vair and purple dyes;
Carve it in doves and pomegranates,
And peacocks with a hundred eyes;
Work it in gold and silver grapes,
In leaves and silver fleurs-de-lys;
Because the birthday of my life

Is come, my love is come to me.

A Bruised Reed Shall He Not Break

I will accept thy will to do and be,
Thy hatred and intolerance of sin,
Thy will at least to love, that burns within
And thirsteth after Me:
So will I render fruitful, blessing still,
The germs and small beginnings in thy heart,
Because thy will cleaves to the better part.—
Alas, I cannot will.
Dost not thou will, poor soul? Yet I receive
The inner unseen longings of the soul,
I guide them turning towards Me; I control
And charm hearts till they grieve:
If thou desire, it yet shall come to pass,
Though thou but wish indeed to choose My love;
For I have power in earth and heaven above.—
I cannot wish, alas!
What, neither choose nor wish to choose? and yet
I still must strive to win thee and constrain:
For thee I hung upon the cross in pain,
How then can I forget?
If thou as yet dost neither love, nor hate,
Nor choose, nor wish,—resign thyself, be still
Till I infuse love, hatred, longing, will.—
I do not deprecate.

A Chill

What can lambkins do
All the keen night through?
Nestle by their woolly mother
The careful ewe.
What can nestlings do
In the nightly dew?
Sleep beneath their mother's wing
Till day breaks anew.
If in a field or tree
There might only be
Such a warm soft sleeping-place
Found for me!

A Chilly Night

I rose at the dead of night
And went to the lattice alone
To look for my Mother's ghost
Where the ghostly moonlight shone.
My friends had failed one by one,
Middleaged, young, and old,
Till the ghosts were warmer to me
Than my friends that had grown cold.
I looked and I saw the ghosts
Dotting plain and mound:
They stood in the blank moonlight
But no shadow lay on the ground;
They spoke without a voice
And they leapt without a sound.
I called: ' O my Mother dear, ' —
I sobbed: ' O my Mother kind,
Make a lonely bed for me
And shelter it from the wind:
' Tell the others not to come
To see me night or day;
But I need not tell my friends
To be sure to keep away. '
My Mother raised her eyes,
They were blank and could not see;
Yet they held me with their stare
While they seemed to look at me.
She opened her mouth and spoke,
I could not hear a word
While my flesh crept on my bones
And every hair was stirred.
She knew that I could not hear
The message that she told

Whether I had long to wait
Or soon should sleep in the mould:
I saw her toss her shadowless hair
And wring her hands in the cold.
I strained to catch her words
And she strained to make me hear,
But never a sound of words
Fell on my straining ear.
From midnight to the cockcrow
I kept my watch in pain
While the subtle ghosts grew subtler
In the sad night on the wane.
From midnight to the cockcrow
I watched till all were gone,
Some to sleep in the shifting sea
And some under turf and stone:
Living had failed and dead had failed
And I was indeed alone.

A Christmas Carol

In the bleak mid-winter
Frosty wind made moan,
Earth stood hard as iron,
Water like a stone;
Snow had fallen, snow on snow,
Snow on snow,
In the bleak mid-winter
Long ago.
Our God, Heaven cannot hold Him,
Nor earth sustain;
Heaven and earth shall flee away
When He comes to reign:
In the bleak mid-winter
A stable-place sufficed
The Lord God Almighty
Jesus Christ.
Enough for Him whom cherubim
Worship night and day,
A breastful of milk
And a mangerful of hay;
Enough for Him whom angels
Fall down before,
The ox and ass and camel
Which adore.
Angels and archangels
May have gathered there.
Cherubim and seraphim
Thronged the air,
But only His mother
In her maiden bliss
Worshipped the Beloved
With a kiss.

What can I give Him,
Poor as I am?
If I were a shepherd
I would bring a lamb,
If I were a wise man
I would do my part, -
Yet what I can I give Him,
Give my heart

A City Plum Is Not A Plum

A city plum is not a plum;
A dumb-bell is no bell, though dumb;
A party rat is not a rat;
A sailor's cat is not a cat;
A soldier's frog is not a frog;
A captain's log is not a log.

A Daughter Of Eve

A fool I was to sleep at noon,
And wake when night is chilly
Beneath the comfortless cold moon;
A fool to pluck my rose too soon,
A fool to snap my lily.
My garden-plot I have not kept;
Faded and all-forsaken,
I weep as I have never wept:
Oh it was summer when I slept,
It's winter now I waken.
Talk what you please of future spring
And sun-warm'd sweet to-morrow:
Stripp'd bare of hope and everything,
No more to laugh, no more to sing,
I sit alone with sorrow.

A Diamond Or A Coal?

A diamond or a coal?
A diamond, if you please:
Who cares about a clumsy coal
Beneath the summer trees?
A diamond or a coal?
A coal, sir, if you please:
One comes to care about the coal
What time the waters freeze.

A Dirge

Why were you born when the snow was falling?
You should have come to the cuckoo's calling
Or when grapes are green in the cluster,
Or, at least, when lithe swallows muster
For their far off flying
From summer dying.
Why did you die when the lambs were cropping?
You should have died at the apples' dropping,
When the grasshopper comes to trouble,
And the wheat-fields are sodden stubble,
And all winds go sighing
For sweet things dying.

A Dream

Once in a dream (for once I dreamed of you)
We stood together in an open field;
Above our heads two swift-winged pigeons wheeled,
Sporting at ease and courting full in view.
When loftier still a broadening darkness flew,
Down-swooping, and a ravenous hawk revealed;
Too weak to fight, too fond to fly, they yield;
So farewell life and love and pleasures new.
Then as their plumes fell fluttering to the ground,
Their snow-white plumage flecked with crimson drops,
I wept, and thought I turned towards you to weep:
But you were gone; while rustling hedgerow tops
Bent in a wind which bore to me a sound
Of far-off piteous bleat of lambs and sheep.

A Farm Walk

The year stood at its equinox
And bluff the North was blowing,
A bleat of lambs came from the flocks,
Green hardy things were growing;
I met a maid with shining locks
Where milky kine were lowing.
She wore a kerchief on her neck,
Her bare arm showed its dimple,
Her apron spread without a speck,
Her air was frank and simple.
She milked into a wooden pail
And sang a country ditty,
An innocent fond lovers' tale,
That was not wise nor witty,
Pathetically rustical,
Too pointless for the city.
She kept in time without a beat
As true as church-bell ringers,
Unless she tapped time with her feet,
Or squeezed it with her fingers;
Her clear unstudied notes were sweet
As many a practised singer's.
I stood a minute out of sight,
Stood silent for a minute
To eye the pail, and creamy white
The frothing milk within it;
To eye the comely milking maid
Herself so fresh and creamy:
'Good day to you,' at last I said;
She turned her head to see me:
'Good day,' she said with lifted head;
Her eyes looked soft and dreamy,
And all the while she milked and milked

The grave cow heavy-laden:
I've seen grand ladies plumed and silked,
But not a sweeter maiden;
But not a sweeter fresher maid
Than this in homely cotton,
Whose pleasant face and silky braid
I have not yet forgotten.
Seven springs have passed since then, as I
Count with a sober sorrow;
Seven springs have come and passed me by,
And spring sets in to-morrow.
I've half a mind to shake myself
Free just for once from London,
To set my work upon the shelf
And leave it done or undone;
To run down by the early train,
Whirl down with shriek and whistle,
And feel the bluff North blow again,
And mark the sprouting thistle
Set up on waste patch of the lane
Its green and tender bristle.
And spy the scarce-blown violet banks,
Crisp primrose leaves and others,
And watch the lambs leap at their pranks
And butt their patient mothers.
Alas, one point in all my plan
My serious thoughts demur to:
Seven years have passed for maid and man,
Seven years have passed for her too;
Perhaps my rose is overblown,
Not rosy or too rosy;
Perhaps in farmhouse of her own
Some husband keeps her cosy,
Where I should show a face unknown.
Good-bye, my wayside posy.

A Frisky Lamb

A frisky lamb
And a frisky child
Playing their pranks
In a cowslip meadow:
The sky all blue
And the air all mild
And the fields all sun
And the lanes half shadow.

A Frog's Fate

Contemptuous of his home beyond
The village and the village-pond,
A large-souled Frog who spurned each byway
Hopped along the imperial highway.
Nor grunting pig nor barking dog
Could disconcert so great a Frog.
The morning dew was lingering yet,
His sides to cool, his tongue to wet:
The night-dew, when the night should come,
A travelled Frog would send him home.
Not so, alas! The wayside grass
Sees him no more: not so, alas!
A broad-wheeled waggon unawares
Ran him down, his joys, his cares.
From dying choke one feeble croak
The Frog's perpetual silence broke: -
'Ye buoyant Frogs, ye great and small,
Even I am mortal after all!
My road to fame turns out a wry way;
I perish on the hideous highway;
Oh for my old familiar byway!'
The choking Frog sobbed and was gone;
The Waggoner strode whistling on.
Unconscious of the carnage done,
Whistling that Waggoner strode on -
Whistling (it may have happened so)
'A froggy would a-wooing go.'
A hypothetic frog trolled he,
Obtuse to a reality.
O rich and poor, O great and small,
Such oversights beset us all.

The mangled Frog abides incog,

The uninteresting actual frog:
The hypothetic frog alone
Is the one frog we dwell upon.

A Green Cornfield

The earth was green, the sky was blue:
I saw and heard one sunny morn
A skylark hang betweent he two,
A singing speck above the corn;
A stage below, in gay accord,
White butterflies danced on the wing,
And still the singing skylark soared,
And silent sank and soared to sing.
The cornfield stretched a tender green
To right and left beside my walks;
I knew he had a nest unseen
Somewhere among the million stalks.
And as I paused to hear his song
While swift the sunny moments slid,
Perhaps his mate sat listening long,
And listened longer than I did.

A Hope Carol

A night was near, a day was near,
Between a day and night
I heard sweet voices calling clear,
Calling me:
I heard a whirr of wing on wing,
But could not see the sight;
I long to see my birds that sing,
I long to see.
Below the stars, beyond the moon,
Between the night and day
I heard a rising falling tune
Calling me:
I long to see the pipes and strings
Whereon such minstrels play;
I long to see each face that sings,
I long to see.
Today or may be not today,
Tonight or not tonight,
All voices that command or pray
Calling me,
Shall kindle in my soul such fire
And in my eyes such light
That I shall see that heart's desire
I long to see.

A House Of Cards

A house of cards
Is neat and small:
Shake the table,
It must fall.
Find the Court cards
One by one;
Raise it, roof it, -
Now it's done: -
Shake the table!
That's the fun.

A Linnet In A Gilded Cage

A linnet in a gilded cage, -
A linnet on a bough, -
In frosty winter one might doubt
Which bird is luckier now.
But let the trees burst out in leaf,
And nests be on the bough,
Which linnet is the luckier bird,
Oh who could doubt it now?

A Motherless Soft Lambkin
A motherless soft lambkin
Along upon a hill;
No mother's fleece to shelter him
And wrap him from the cold: -
I'll run to him and comfort him,
I'll fetch him, that I will;
I'll care for him and feed him
Until he's strong and bold.

A Pause

They made the chamber sweet with flowers and leaves,
And the bed sweet with flowers on which I lay;
While my soul, love-bound, loitered on its way.
I did not hear the birds about the eaves,
Nor hear the reapers talk among the sheaves:
Only my soul kept watch from day to day,
My thirsty soul kept watch for one away:--
Perhaps he loves, I thought, remembers, grieves.
At length there came the step upon the stair,
Upon the lock the old familiar hand:
Then first my spirit seemed to scent the air
Of Paradise; then first the tardy sand
Of time ran golden; and I felt my hair
Put on a glory,and my soul expand.

A Pause Of Thought

I looked for that which is not, nor can be,
And hope deferred made my heart sick in truth:
But years must pass before a hope of youth
Is resigned utterly.
I watched and waited with a steadfast will:
And though the object seemed to flee away
That I so longed for, ever day by day
I watched and waited still.
Sometimes I said: This thing shall be no more;
My expectation wearies and shall cease;
I will resign it now and be at peace:
Yet never gave it o'er.
Sometimes I said: It is an empty name
I long for; to a name why should I give
The peace of all the days I have to live?—
Yet gave it all the same.
Alas, thou foolish one! alike unfit
For healthy joy and salutary pain:
Thou knowest the chase useless, and again
Turnest to follow it.

A Peal Of Bells

Strike the bells wantonly,
Tinkle tinkle well;
Bring me wine, bring me flowers,
Ring the silver bell.
All my lamps burn scented oil,
Hung on laden orange-trees,
Whose shadowed foliage is the foil
To golden lamps and oranges.
Heap my golden plates with fruit,
Golden fruit, fresh-plucked and ripe;
Strike the bells and breathe the pipe;
Shut out showers from summer hours—
Silence that complaining lute—
Shut out thinking, shut out pain,
From hours that cannot come again.
Strike the bells solemnly,
Ding dong deep:
My friend is passing to his bed,
Fast asleep;
There's plaited linen round his head,
While foremost go his feet—
His feet that cannot carry him.
My feast's a show, my lights are dim;
Be still, your music is not sweet,—
There is no music more for him:
His lights are out, his feast is done;
His bowl that sparkled to the brim
Is drained, is broken, cannot hold;
My blood is chill, his blood is cold;
His death is full, and mine begun.

A Pin Has A Head, But Has No Hair

A pin has a head, but has no hair;
A clock has a face, but no mouth there;
Needles have eyes, but they cannot see;
A fly has a trunk without lock or key;
A timepiece may lose, but cannot win;
A corn-field dimples without a chin;
A hill has no leg, but has a foot;
A wine-glass a stem, but not a root;
A watch has hands, but no thumb or finger;
A boot has a tongue, but is no singer;
Rivers run, though they have no feet;
A saw has teeth, but it does not eat;
Ash-trees have keys, yet never a lock;
And baby crows, without being a cock.

A Pocket Handkerchief To Hem
A pocket handkerchief to hem -
Oh dear, oh dear, oh dear!
How many stitches it will take
Before it's done, I fear.
Yet set a stitch and then a stitch,
And stitch and stitch away,
Till stitch by stitch the hem is done -
And after work is play!

A Portrait

I

She gave up beauty in her tender youth,
Gave all her hope and joy and pleasant ways;
She covered up her eyes lest they should gaze
On vanity, and chose the bitter truth.
Harsh towards herself, towards others full of ruth,
Servant of servants, little known to praise,
Long prayers and fasts trenched on her nights and days:
She schooled herself to sights and sounds uncouth
That with the poor and stricken she might make
A home, until the least of all sufficed
Her wants; her own self learned she to forsake,
Counting all earthly gain but hurt and loss.
So with calm will she chose and bore the cross
And hated all for love of Jesus Christ.

II

They knelt in silent anguish by her bed,
And could not weep; but calmly there she lay.
All pain had left her; and the sun's last ray
Shone through upon her, warming into red
The shady curtains. In her heart she said:
'Heaven opens; I leave these and go away;
The Bridegroom calls,—shall the Bride seek to stay?'
Then low upon her breast she bowed her head.
O lily flower, O gem of priceless worth,
O dove with patient voice and patient eyes,
O fruitful vine amid a land of dearth,
O maid replete with loving purities,
Thou bowedst down thy head with friends on earth
To raise it with the saints in Paradise.

A Riddle

There is one that has a head without an eye,
And there's one that has an eye without a head.
You may find the answer if you try;
And when all is said,
Half the answer hangs upon a thread.

A Ring Posy
Jess and Jill are pretty girls,
Plump and well to do,
In a cloud of windy curls:
Yet I know who
Loves me more than curls or pearls.
I'm not pretty, not a bit—
Thin and sallow-pale;
When I trudge along the street
I don't need a veil:
Yet I have one fancy hit.
Jess and Jill can trill and sing
With a flute-like voice,
Dance as light as bird on wing,
Laugh for careless joys:
Yet it's I who wear the ring.
Jess and Jill will mate some day,
Surely, surely:
Ripen on to June through May,
While the sun shines make their hay,
Slacken steps demurely:
Yet even there I lead the way.

A Ring Upon Her Finger

A ring upon her finger,
Walks the bride,
With the bridegroom tall and handsome
At her side.
A veil upon her forehead
Walks the bride,
With the bridegroom proud and merry
At her side.
Fling flowers beneath the footsteps
Of the bride;
Fling flowers before the bridegroom
At her side.

A Rose Has Thorns As Well As Honey

A rose has thorns as well as honey,
I'll not have her for love or money;
An iris grows so straight and fine,
That she shall be no friend of mine;
Snowdrops like the snow would chill me;
Nightshade would caress and kill me;
Crocus like a spear would fright me;
Dragon's-mouth might bark or bite me;
Convolvulus but blooms to die;
A wind-flower suggests a sigh;
Love-lies-bleeding makes me sad;
And poppy-juice would drive me mad: -
But give me holly, bold and jolly,
Honest, prickly, shining holly;
Pluck me holly leaf and berry
For the day when I make merry.

I, a princess, king-descended, decked with jewels, gilded, drest,

Would rather be a peasant with her baby at her breast,
For all I shine so like the sun, and am purple like the west.
Two and two my guards behind, two and two before,
Two and two on either hand, they guard me evermore;
Me, poor dove, that must not coo—eagle that must not soar.
All my fountains cast up perfumes, all my gardens grow
Scented woods and foreign spices, with all flowers in blow
That are costly, out of season as the seasons go.
All my walls are lost in mirrors, whereupon I trace
Self to right hand, self to left hand, self in every place,
Self-same solitary figure, self-same seeking face.
Then I have an ivory chair high to sit upon,
Almost like my father's chair, which is an ivory throne;
There I sit uplift and upright, there I sit alone.
Alone by day, alone by night, alone days without end;
My father and my mother give me treasures, search and spend—
O my father! O my mother! have you ne'er a friend?
As I am a lofty princess, so my father is
A lofty king, accomplished in all kingly subtilties,
Holding in his strong right hand world-kingdoms' balances.
He has quarrelled with his neighbours, he has scourged his foes;
Vassal counts and princes follow where his pennon goes,
Long-descended valiant lords whom the vulture knows,

On whose track the vulture swoops,
when they ride in state
To break the strength of armies
and topple down the great:
Each of these my courteous servant, none of these my mate.
My father counting up his strength sets down with equal pen
So many head of cattle, head of horses, head of men;
These for slaughter, these for breeding, with the how and when.

Some to work on roads, canals; some to man his ships;
Some to smart in mines beneath sharp overseers' whips;
Some to trap fur-beasts in lands where utmost winter nips.
Once it came into my heart, and whelmed me like a flood,
That these too are men and women, human flesh and blood;
Men with hearts and men with souls, though trodden down like mud.
Our feasting was not glad that night, our music was not gay:
On my mother's graceful head I marked a thread of grey,
My father frowning at the fare seemed every dish to weigh.
I sat beside them sole princess in my exalted place,
My ladies and my gentlemen stood by me on the dais:
A mirror showed me I look old and haggard in the face;
It showed me that my ladies all are fair to gaze upon,
Plump, plenteous-haired, to every one love's secret lore is known,
They laugh by day, they sleep by night; ah me, what is a throne?
The singing men and women sang that night as usual,
The dancers danced in pairs and sets, but music had a fall,
A melancholy windy fall as at a funeral.
Amid the toss of torches to my chamber back we swept;
My ladies loosed my golden chain; meantime
I could have wept

To think of some in galling chains whether they waked or slept.
I took my bath of scented milk, delicately waited on,
They burned sweet things for my delight, cedar and cinnamon,
They lit my shaded silver lamp, and left me there alone.
A day went by, a week went by. One day I heard it said:
'Men are clamouring, women, children, clamouring to be fed;
Men like famished dogs are howling in the streets for bread.'
So two whispered by my door, not thinking I could hear,
Vulgar naked truth, ungarnished for a royal ear;
Fit for cooping in the background, not to stalk so near.
But I strained my utmost sense to catch this truth, and mark:

'There are families out grazing like cattle in the park.'
'A pair of peasants must be saved even if we build an ark.'
A merry jest, a merry laugh, each strolled upon his way;
One was my page, a lad I reared and bore with day by day;
One was my youngest maid as sweet and white as cream in May.
Other footsteps followed softly with a weightier tramp;
Voices said: 'Picked soldiers have been summoned from the camp
To quell these base-born ruffians who make free to howl and stamp.'
'Howl and stamp?' one answered: 'They made free to hurl a stone
At the minister's state coach, well aimed and stoutly thrown.'
'There's work then for the soldiers, for this rank crop must be mown.'
'One I saw, a poor old fool with ashes on his head,
Whimpering because a girl had snatched his crust of bread:
Then he dropped; when some one raised him,
it turned out he was dead.'
'After us the deluge,' was retorted with a laugh:

'If bread's the staff of life, they must walk without a staff.'
'While I've a loaf they're welcome to my blessing and the chaff.'
These passed. The king: stand up. Said my father with a smile:
'Daughter mine, your mother comes to sit with you awhile,
She's sad to-day, and who but you her sadness can beguile?'
He too left me. Shall I touch my harp now while I wait,—
(I hear them doubling guard below before our palace gate—)
Or shall I work the last gold stitch into my veil of state;
Or shall my woman stand and read some unimpassioned scene,
There's music of a lulling sort in words that pause between;
Or shall she merely fan me while I wait here for the queen?
Again I caught my father's voice in sharp word of command:
'Charge!' a clash of steel: 'Charge again, the rebels stand.
Smite and spare not, hand to hand;
smite and spare not, hand to hand.'
There swelled a tumult at the gate, high voices waxing higher;
A flash of red reflected light lit the cathedral spire;
I heard a cry for faggots, then I heard a yell for fire.

'Sit and roast there with your meat,
sit and bake there with your bread,
You who sat to see us starve,' one shrieking woman said:
'Sit on your throne and roast with your crown upon your head.'
Nay, this thing will I do, while my mother tarrieth,
I will take my fine spun gold, but not to sew therewith,
I will take my gold and gems, and rainbow fan and wreath;
With a ransom in my lap, a king's ransom in my hand,
I will go down to this people, will stand face to face, will stand
Where they curse king, queen, and princess
of this cursed land.
They shall take all to buy them bread, take all
I have to give;
I, if I perish, perish; they to-day shall eat and live;
I, if I perish, perish; that's the goal I half conceive:
Once to speak before the world, rend bare
my heart and show
The lesson I have learned which is death, is life,
to know.I, if I perish, perish; in the name of
God I go.

A Study (A Soul)

She stands as pale as Parian statues stand;
Like Cleopatra when she turned at bay,
And felt her strength above the Roman sway,
And felt the aspic writhing in her hand.
Her face is steadfast toward the shadowy land,
For dim beyond it looms the light of day;
Her feet are steadfast; all the arduous way
That foot-track hath not wavered on the sand.
She stands there like a beacon thro' the night,
A pale clear beacon where the storm-drift is;
She stands alone, a wonder deathly white;
She stands there patient, nerved with inner might,
Indomitable in her feebleness,
Her face and will athirst against the light.

A Summer Wish

Live all thy sweet life through,
Sweet Rose, dew-sprent,
Drop down thine evening dew
To gather it anew
When day is bright:
I fancy thou wast meant
Chiefly to give delight.
Sing in the silent sky,
Glad soaring bird;
Sing out thy notes on high
To sunbeam straying by
Or passing cloud;
Heedless if thou art heard
Sing thy full song aloud.
Oh that it were with me
As with the flower;
Blooming on its own tree
For butterfly and bee
Its summer morns:
That I might bloom mine hour
A rose in spite of thorns.
Oh that my work were done
As birds' that soar
Rejoicing in the sun:
That when my time is run
And daylight too,
I so might rest once more
Cool with refreshing dew.

A Testimony

I said of laughter: it is vain.
Of mirth I said: what profits it?
Therefore I found a book, and writ
Therein how ease and also pain,
How health and sickness, every one
Is vanity beneath the sun.
Man walks in a vain shadow; he
Disquieteth himself in vain.
The things that were shall be again;
The rivers do not fill the sea,
But turn back to their secret source;
The winds too turn upon their course.
Our treasures moth and rust corrupt,
Or thieves break through and steal, or they
Make themselves wings and fly away.
One man made merry as he supped,
Nor guessed how when that night grew dim,
His soul would be required of him.
We build our houses on the sand
Comely withoutside and within;
But when the winds and rains begin
To beat on them, they cannot stand;
They perish, quickly overthrown,
Loose from the very basement stone.
All things are vanity, I said:
Yea vanity of vanities.
The rich man dies; and the poor dies:
The worm feeds sweetly on the dead.
Whate'er thou lackest, keep this trust:
All in the end shall have but dust.
The one inheritance, which best
And worst alike shall find and share:
The wicked cease from troubling there,

And there the weary are at rest;

There all the wisdom of the wise
Is vanity of vanities.
Man flourishes as a green leaf,
And as a leaf doth pass away;
Or as a shade that cannot stay,
And leaves no track, his course is brief:
Yet doth man hope and fear and plan
Till he is dead:—oh foolish man!
Our eyes cannot be satisfied
With seeing, nor our ears be filled
With hearing: yet we plant and build
And buy and make our borders wide;
We gather wealth, we gather care,
But know not who shall be our heir.
Why should we hasten to arise
So early, and so late take rest?
Our labour is not good; our best
Hopes fade; our heart is stayed on lies:
Verily, we sow wind; and we
Shall reap the whirlwind, verily.
He who hath little shall not lack;
He who hath plenty shall decay:
Our fathers went; we pass away;
Our children follow on our track:
So generations fail, and so
They are renewed, and come and go.
The earth is fattened with our dead;
She swallows more and doth not cease:
Therefore her wine and oil increase
And her sheaves are not numbered;
Therefore her plants are green, and all
Her pleasant trees lusty and tall.
Therefore the maidens cease to sing,
And the young men are very sad;
Therefore the sowing is not glad,

And mournful is the harvesting.

Of high and low, of great and small,
Vanity is the lot of all.
A King dwelt in Jerusalem;
He was the wisest man on earth;
He had all riches from his birth,
And pleasures till he tired of them;
Then, having tested all things, he
Witnessed that all are vanity.

A Toadstool Comes Up In A Night

A toadstool comes up in a night, -
Learn the lesson, little folk: -
An oak grows on a hundred years,
But then it is an oak.

A Triad

Three sang of love together: one with lips
Crimson, with cheeks and bosom in a glow,
Flushed to the yellow hair and finger-tips;
And one there sang who soft and smooth as snow
Bloomed like a tinted hyacinth at a show;
And one was blue with famine after love,
Who like a harpstring snapped rang harsh and low
The burden of what those were singing of.
One shamed herself in love; one temperately
Grew gross in soulless love, a sluggish wife;
One famished died for love. Thus two of three
Took death for love and won him after strife;
One droned in sweetness like a fattened bee:
All on the threshold, yet all short of life.

A White Hen Sitting

A white hen sitting
On white eggs three:
Next, three speckled chickens
As plump as plump can be.
An owl, and a hawk,
And a bat come to see:
But chicks beneath their mother's wing
Squat safe as safe can be.

A Year's Windfalls
On the wind of January
Down flits the snow,
Travelling from the frozen North
As cold as it can blow.
Poor robin redbreast,
Look where he comes;
Let him in to feel your fire,
And toss him of your crumbs.
On the wind in February
Snowflakes float still,
Half inclined to turn to rain,
Nipping, dripping, chill.
Then the thaws swell the streams,
And swollen rivers swell the sea:—
If the winter ever ends
How pleasant it will be!
In the wind of windy March
The catkins drop down,
Curly, caterpillar-like,
Curious green and brown.
With concourse of nest-building birds
And leaf-buds by the way,
We begin to think of flowers

And life and nuts some day.
With the gusts of April
Rich fruit-tree blossoms fall,
On the hedged-in orchard-green,
From the southern wall.
Apple-trees and pear-trees
Shed petals white or pink,
Plum-trees and peach-trees;
While sharp showers sink and sink.
Little brings the May breeze
Beside pure scent of flowers,
While all things wax and nothing wanes

In lengthening daylight hours.
Across the hyacinth beds
The wind lags warm and sweet,
Across the hawthorn tops,
Across the blades of wheat.
In the wind of sunny June
Thrives the red rose crop,
Every day fresh blossoms blow
While the first leaves drop;
White rose and yellow rose
And moss-rose choice to find,
And the cottage cabbage-rose
Not one whit behind.
On the blast of scorched July
Drives the pelting hail,
From thunderous lightning-clouds, that blot
Blue heaven grown lurid-pale.
Weedy waves are tossed ashore,
Sea-things strange to sight
Gasp upon the barren shore
And fade away in light.
In the parching August wind
Corn-fields bow the head,
Sheltered in round valley depths,

On low hills outspread.
Early leaves drop loitering down
Weightless on the breeze,
First fruits of the year's decay
From the withering trees.
In brisk wind of September
The heavy-headed fruits
Shake upon their bending boughs
And drop from the shoots;
Some glow golden in the sun,
Some show green and streaked,
Some set forth a purple bloom,
Some blush rosy-cheeked.

In strong blast of October
At the equinox,
Stirred up in his hollow bed
Broad ocean rocks;
Plunge the ships on his bosom,
Leaps and plunges the foam,—
It's oh! for mothers' sons at sea,
That they were safe at home.
In slack wind of November
The fog forms and shifts;
All the world comes out again
When the fog lifts.
Loosened from their sapless twigs
Leaves drop with every gust;
Drifting, rustling, out of sight
In the damp or dust.
Last of all, December,
The year's sands nearly run,
Speeds on the shortest day,
Curtails the sun;
With its bleak raw wind
Lays the last leaves low,
Brings back the nightly frosts,
Brings back the snow.

Advent

This Advent moon shines cold and clear,
These Advent nights are long;
Our lamps have burned year after year
And still their flame is strong.
'Watchman, what of the night?' we cry,
Heart-sick with hope deferred:
'No speaking signs are in the sky,'
Is still the watchman's word.
The Porter watches at the gate,
The servants watch within;
The watch is long betimes and late,
The prize is slow to win.
'Watchman, what of the night?' But still
His answer sounds the same:
'No daybreak tops the utmost hill,
Nor pale our lamps of flame.'
One to another hear them speak
The patient virgins wise:
'Surely He is not far to seek'—
'All night we watch and rise.'
'The days are evil looking back,
The coming days are dim;
Yet count we not His promise slack,
But watch and wait for Him.'
One with another, soul with soul,
They kindle fire from fire:
'Friends watch us who have touched the goal.'
'They urge us, come up higher.'
'With them shall rest our waysore feet,
With them is built our home,
With Christ.'—'They sweet, but He most sweet,
Sweeter than honeycomb.'

There no more parting, no more pain,
The distant ones brought near,
The lost so long are found again,

Long lost but longer dear:
Eye hath not seen, ear hath not heard,
Nor heart conceived that rest,
With them our good things long deferred,
With Jesus Christ our Best.
We weep because the night is long,
We laugh for day shall rise,
We sing a slow contented song
And knock at Paradise.
Weeping we hold Him fast, Who wept
For us, we hold Him fast;
And will not let Him go except
He bless us first or last.
Weeping we hold Him fast to-night;
We will not let Him go
Till daybreak smite our wearied sight
And summer smite the snow:
Then figs shall bud, and dove with dove
Shall coo the livelong day;
Then He shall say, 'Arise, My love,
My fair one, come away.'

After Death

The curtains were half drawn, the floor was swept
And strewn with rushes, rosemary and may
Lay thick upon the bed on which I lay,
Where through the lattice ivy-shadows crept.
He leaned above me, thinking that I slept
And could not hear him; but I heard him say:
'Poor child, poor child:' and as he turned away
Came a deep silence, and I knew he wept.
He did not touch the shroud, or raise the fold
That hid my face, or take my hand in his,
Or ruffle the smooth pillows for my head:
He did not love me living; but once dead
He pitied me; and very sweet it is
To know he still is warm though I am cold.

After This The Judgement

As eager homebound traveller to the goal,
Or steadfast seeker on an unsearched main,
Or martyr panting for an aureole,
My fellow-pilgrims pass me, and attain
That hidden mansion of perpetual peace
Where keen desire and hope dwell free from pain:
That gate stands open of perennial ease;
I view the glory till I partly long,
Yet lack the fire of love which quickens these.
O passing Angel, speed me with a song,
A melody of heaven to reach my heart
And rouse me to the race and make me strong;
Till in such music I take up my part
Swelling those Hallelujahs full of rest,
One, tenfold, hundredfold, with heavenly art,
Fulfilling north and south and east and west,
Thousand, ten thousandfold, innumerable,
All blent in one yet each one manifest;
Each one distinguished and beloved as well
As if no second voice in earth or heaven
Were lifted up the Love of God to tell.
Ah, Love of God, which Thine own Self hast given
To me most poor, and made me rich in love,
Love that dost pass the tenfold seven times seven,
Draw Thou mine eyes, draw Thou my heart above,
My treasure ad my heart store Thou in Thee,
Brood over me with yearnings of a dove;
Be Husband, Brother, closest Friend to me;
Love me as very mother loves her son,
Her sucking firstborn fondled on her knee:
Yea, more than mother loves her little one;
For, earthly, even a mother may forget
And feel no pity for its piteous moan;

But thou, O Love of God, remember yet,
Through the dry desert, through the waterflood
(Life, death) until the Great White Throne is set.
If now I am sick in chewing the bitter cud
Of sweet past sin, though solaced by Thy grace
And ofttimes strengthened by Thy Flesh and Blood,

How shall I then stand up before Thy face
When from Thine eyes repentance shall be hid
And utmost Justice stand in Mercy's place:
When every sin I thought or spoke or did
Shall meet me at the inexorable bar,
And there be no man standing in the mid
To plead for me; while star fallen after star
With heaven and earth are like a ripened shock,
And all time's mighty works and wonders are
Consumed as in a moment; when no rock
Remains to fall on me, no tree to hide,
But I stand all creation's gazing-stock
Exposed and comfortless on every side,
Placed trembling in the final balances
Whose poise this hour, this moment, must be tried?—
Ah Love of God, if greater love than this
Hath no man, that a man die for his friend,
And if such love of love Thine Own Love is,
Plead with Thyself, with me, before the end;
Redeem me from the irrevocable past;
Pitch Thou Thy Presence round me to defend;
Yea seek with pierced feet, yea hold me fast
With pierced hands whose wounds were made by love;
Not what I am, remember what Thou wast
When darkness hid from Thee Thy heavens above,
And sin Thy Father's Face, while thou didst drink
The bitter cup of death, didst taste thereof
For every man; while Thou wast nigh to sink
Beneath the intense intolerable rod,
Grown sick of love; not what I am, but think

Thy Life then ransomed mine, my God, my God.

All the bells were ringing
And all the birds were singing,
When Molly sat down crying
For her broken doll:
O you silly Moll!
Sobbing and sighing
For a broken doll,
When all the bells are ringing
And all the birds are singing.

Aloof

THE irresponsive silence of the land,
    The irresponsive sounding of the sea,
    Speak both one message of one sense to me:--
Aloof, aloof, we stand aloof, so stand
Thou too aloof, bound with the flawless band
    Of inner solitude; we bind not thee;
    But who from thy self-chain shall set thee free?
What heart shall touch thy heart? What hand thy hand?
And I am sometimes proud and sometimes meek,
    And sometimes I remember days of old
When fellowship seem'd not so far to seek,
    And all the world and I seem'd much less cold,
    And at the rainbow's foot lay surely gold,
And hope felt strong, and life itself not weak.

Amen

It is over. What is over?
Nay, now much is over truly!—
Harvest days we toiled to sow for;
Now the sheaves are gathered newly,
Now the wheat is garnered duly.
It is finished. What is finished?
Much is finished known or unknown:
Lives are finished; time diminished;
Was the fallow field left unsown?
Will these buds be always unblown?
It suffices. What suffices?
All suffices reckoned rightly:
Spring shall bloom where now the ice is,
Roses make the bramble sightly,
And the quickening sun shine brightly,
And the latter wind blow lightly,
And my garden teem with spices.
Maiden-Song
Long ago and long ago,
And long ago still,
There dwelt three merry maidens
Upon a distant hill.
One was tall Meggan,
And one was dainty May,
But one was fair Margaret,
More fair than I can say,
Long ago and long ago.
When Meggan plucked the thorny rose,
And when May pulled the brier,
Half the birds would swoop to see,
Half the beasts draw nigher;
Half the fishes of the streams
Would dart up to admire:

But when Margaret plucked a flag-flower,
Or poppy hot aflame,

All the beasts and all the birds
And all the fishes came
To her hand more soft than snow.
Strawberry leaves and May-dew
In brisk morning air,
Strawberry leaves and May-dew
Make maidens fair.
'I go for strawberry leaves,'
Meggan said one day:
'Fair Margaret can bide at home,
But you come with me, May;
Up the hill and down the hill,
Along the winding way
You and I are used to go.'
So these two fair sisters
Went with innocent will
Up the hill and down again,
And round the homestead hill:
While the fairest sat at home,
Margaret like a queen,
Like a blush-rose, like the moon
In her heavenly sheen,
Fragrant-breathed as milky cow
Or field of blossoming bean,
Graceful as an ivy bough
Born to cling and lean;
Thus she sat to sing and sew.
When she raised her lustrous eyes
A beast peeped at the door;
When she downward cast her eyes
A fish gasped on the floor;
When she turned away her eyes
A bird perched on the sill,
Warbling out its heart of love,

Warbling warbling still,
With pathetic pleadings low.
Light-foot May with Meggan
Sought the choicest spot,

Clothed with thyme-alternate grass:
Then, while day waxed hot,
Sat at ease to play and rest,
A gracious rest and play;
The loveliest maidens near or far,
When Margaret was away,
Who sat at home to sing and sew.
Sun-glow flushed their comely cheeks,
Wind-play tossed their hair,
Creeping things among the grass
Stroked them here and there;
Meggan piped a merry note,
A fitful wayward lay,
While shrill as bird on topmost twig
Piped merry May;
Honey-smooth the double flow.
Sped a herdsman from the vale,
Mounting like a flame,
All on fire to hear and see,
With floating locks he came.
Looked neither north nor south,
Neither east nor west,
But sat him down at Meggan's feet
As love-bird on his nest,
And wooed her with a silent awe,
With trouble not expressed;
She sang the tears into his eyes,
The heart out of his breast:
So he loved her, listening so.
She sang the heart out of his breast,
The words out of his tongue;
Hand and foot and pulse he paused

Till her song was sung.
Then he spoke up from his place
Simple words and true:
'Scanty goods have I to give,
Scanty skill to woo;
But I have a will to work,
And a heart for you:

Bid me stay or bid me go.'
Then Meggan mused within herself:
'Better be first with him,
Than dwell where fairer Margaret sits,
Who shines my brightness dim,
For ever second where she sits,
However fair I be:
I will be lady of his love,
And he shall worship me;
I will be lady of his herds
And stoop to his degree,
At home where kids and fatlings grow.'
Sped a shepherd from the height
Headlong down to look,
(White lambs followed, lured by love
Of their shepherd's crook):
He turned neither east nor west,
Neither north nor south,
But knelt right down to May, for love
Of her sweet-singing mouth;
Forgot his flocks, his panting flocks
In parching hill-side drouth;
Forgot himself for weal or woe.
Trilled her song and swelled her song
With maiden coy caprice
In a labyrinth of throbs,
Pauses, cadences;
Clear-noted as a dropping brook,
Soft-noted like the bees,

Wild-noted as the shivering wind
Forlorn through forest trees:
Love-noted like the wood-pigeon
Who hides herself for love,
Yet cannot keep her secret safe,
But coos and coos thereof:
Thus the notes rang loud or low.
He hung breathless on her breath;
Speechless, who listened well;

Could not speak or think or wish
Till silence broke the spell.
Then he spoke, and spread his hands,
Pointing here and there:
'See my sheep and see the lambs,
Twin lambs which they bare.
All myself I offer you,
All my flocks and care,
Your sweet song hath moved me so.'
In her fluttered heart young May
Mused a dubious while:
'If he loves me as he says'—
Her lips curved with a smile:
'Where Margaret shines like the sun
I shine but like a moon;
If sister Meggan makes her choice
I can make mine as soon;
At cockcrow we were sister-maids,
We may be brides at noon.'
Said Meggan, 'Yes;' May said not 'No.'
Fair Margaret stayed alone at home,
Awhile she sang her song,
Awhile sat silent, then she thought:
'My sisters loiter long.'
That sultry noon had waned away,
Shadows had waxen great:
'Surely,' she thought within herself,

'My sisters loiter late.'
She rose, and peered out at the door,
With patient heart to wait,
And heard a distant nightingale
Complaining of its mate;
Then down the garden slope she walked,
Down to the garden gate,
Leaned on the rail and waited so.
The slope was lightened by her eyes
Like summer lightning fair,
Like rising of the haloed moon
Lightened her glimmering hair,

While her face lightened like the sun
Whose dawn is rosy white.
Thus crowned with maiden majesty
She peered into the night,
Looked up the hill and down the hill,
To left hand and to right,
Flashing like fire-flies to and fro.
Waiting thus in weariness
She marked the nightingale
Telling, if any one would heed,
Its old complaining tale.
Then lifted she her voice and sang,
Answering the bird:
Then lifted she her voice and sang,
Such notes were never heard
From any bird when Spring's in blow.
The king of all that country
Coursing far, coursing near,
Curbed his amber-bitted steed,
Coursed amain to hear;
All his princes in his train,
Squire, and knight, and peer,
With his crown upon his head,
His sceptre in his hand,

Down he fell at Margaret's knees
Lord king of all that land,
To her highness bending low.
Every beast and bird and fish
Came mustering to the sound,
Every man and every maid
From miles of country round:
Meggan on her herdsman's arm,
With her shepherd May,
Flocks and herds trooped at their heels
Along the hill-side way;
No foot too feeble for the ascent,
Not any head too grey;
Some were swift and none were slow.

So Margaret sang her sisters home
In their marriage mirth;
Sang free birds out of the sky,
Beasts along the earth,
Sang up fishes of the deep—
All breathing things that move
Sang from far and sang from near
To her lovely love;
Sang together friend and foe;
Sang a golden-bearded king
Straightway to her feet,
Sang him silent where he knelt
In eager anguish sweet.
But when the clear voice died away,
When longest echoes died,
He stood up like a royal man
And claimed her for his bride.
So three maids were wooed and won
In a brief May-tide,
Long ago and long ago.

JESSIE CAMERON

'Jessie, Jessie Cameron,

Hear me but this once,' quoth he.
'Good luck go with you, neighbor's son,
But I'm no mate for you,' quoth she.
Day was verging toward the night
There beside the moaning sea,
Dimness overtook the light
There where the breakers be.
'O Jessie, Jessie Cameron,
I have loved you long and true.'—
'Good luck go with you, neighbor's son,
But I'm no mate for you.'
She was a careless, fearless girl,
And made her answer plain,
Outspoken she to earl or churl,
Kindhearted in the main,
But somewhat heedless with her tongue,
And apt at causing pain;

A mirthful maiden she and young,
Most fair for bliss or bane.
'Oh, long ago I told you so,
I tell you so to-day:
Go you your way, and let me go
Just my own free way.'
The sea swept in with moan and foam,
Quickening the stretch of sand;
They stood almost in sight of home;
He strove to take her hand.
'Oh, can't you take your answer then,
And won't you understand?
For me you're not the man of men,
I've other plans are planned.
You're good for Madge, or good for Cis,
Or good for Kate, may be:
But what's to me the good of this
While you're not good for me?'
They stood together on the beach,

They two alone,
And louder waxed his urgent speech,
His patience almost gone:
'Oh, say but one kind word to me,
Jessie, Jessie Cameron.'—
'I'd be too proud to beg,' quoth she,
And pride was in her tone.
And pride was in her lifted head,
And in her angry eye
And in her foot, which might have fled,
But would not fly.
Some say that he had gipsy blood;
That in his heart was guile:
Yet he had gone through fire and flood
Only to win her smile.
Some say his grandam was a witch,
A black witch from beyond the Nile,
Who kept an image in a niche
And talked with it the while.
And by her hut far down the lane

Some say they would not pass at night,
Lest they should hear an unked strain
Or see an unked sight.
Alas, for Jessie Cameron!—
The sea crept moaning, moaning nigher:
She should have hastened to begone,—
The sea swept higher, breaking by her:
She should have hastened to her home
While yet the west was flushed with fire,
But now her feet are in the foam,
The sea-foam, sweeping higher.
O mother, linger at your door,
And light your lamp to make it plain,
But Jessie she comes home no more,
No more again.
They stood together on the strand,

They only, each by each;
Home, her home, was close at hand,
Utterly out of reach.
Her mother in the chimney nook
Heard a startled sea-gull screech,
But never turned her head to look
Towards the darkening beach:
Neighbours here and neighbours there
Heard one scream, as if a bird
Shrilly screaming cleft the air:—
That was all they heard.
Jessie she comes home no more,
Comes home never;
Her lover's step sounds at his door
No more forever.
And boats may search upon the sea
And search along the river,
But none know where the bodies be:
Sea-winds that shiver,
Sea-birds that breast the blast,
Sea-waves swelling,
Keep the secret first and last
Of their dwelling.

Whether the tide so hemmed them round
With its pitiless flow,
That when they would have gone they found
No way to go;
Whether she scorned him to the last
With words flung to and fro,
Or clung to him when hope was past,
None will ever know:
Whether he helped or hindered her,
Threw up his life or lost it well,
The troubled sea, for all its stir
Finds no voice to tell.
Only watchers by the dying

Have thought they heard one pray
Wordless, urgent; and replying
One seem to say him nay:
And watchers by the dead have heard
A windy swell from miles away,
With sobs and screams, but not a word
Distinct for them to say:
And watchers out at sea have caught
Glimpse of a pale gleam here or there,
Come and gone as quick as thought,
Which might be hand or hair.

Amor Mundi

'Oh, where are you going with your love-locks flowing
On the west wind blowing along this valley track?'
'The downhill path is easy, come with me an' it please ye,
We shall escape the uphill by never turning back.'
So they two went together in glowing August weather,
The honey-breathing heather lay to their left and right;
And dear she was to doat on, her swift feet seemed to float on
The air like soft twin pigeons too sportive to alight.
'Oh, what is that in heaven where grey cloud-flakes are seven,
Where blackest clouds hang riven just at the rainy skirt?'
'Oh, that's a meteor sent us, a message dumb, portentous,—
An undeciphered solemn signal of help or hurt.'
'Oh, what is that glides quickly where velvet flowers grow thickly,
Their scent comes rich and sickly?'—'A scaled and hooded worm.'
'Oh, what's that in the hollow, so pale I quake to follow?'
'Oh, that's a thin dead body which waits th' eternal term.'
'Turn again, O my sweetest,—turn again, false and fleetest:
This way whereof thou weetest I fear is hell's own track.'
'Nay, too steep for hill-mounting,—nay, too late for cost-counting:
This downhill path is easy, but there's no turning back.'

An Apple-Gathering

I plucked pink blossoms from mine apple tree
And wore them all that evening in my hair:
Then in due season when I went to see
I found no apples there.
With dangling basket all along the grass
As I had come I went the selfsame track:
My neighbours mocked me while they saw me pass
So empty-handed back.
Lilian and Lilias smiled in trudging by,
Their heaped-up basket teazed me like a jeer;
Sweet-voiced they sang beneath the sunset sky,
Their mother's home was near.
Plump Gertrude passed me with her basket full,
A stronger hand than hers helped it along;
A voice talked with her thro' the shadows cool
More sweet to me than song.
Ah Willie, Willie, was my love less worth
Than apples with their green leaves piled above?
I counted rosiest apples on the earth
Of far less worth than love.
So once it was with me you stooped to talk
Laughing and listening in this very lane:
To think that by this way we used to walk
We shall not walk again!
I let my neighbours pass me, ones and twos
And groups; the latest said the night grew chill,
And hastened: but I loitered, while the dews
Fell fast I loitered still.

An Echo From Willowood
"Oh Ye, All Ye That Walk in Willowwood"
Two gaz'd into a pool, he gaz'd and she,
Not hand in hand, yet heart in heart, I think,

Pale and reluctant on the water's brink
AS on the brink of parting which must be.
Each eyed the other's aspect, she and he,
Each felt one hungering heart leap up and sink,
Each tasted bitterness which both must drink,
There on the brink of life's dividing sea.
Lilies upon the surface, deep below
Two wistful faces craving each for each,
Resolute and reluctant without speech:—
A sudden ripple made the faces flow
One moment join'd, to vanish out of reach:
So these hearts join'd, and ah! were parted so.

An Emerald Is As Green As Grass

An emerald is as green as grass;
A ruby red as blood;
A sapphire shines as blue as heaven;
A flint lies in the mud.
A diamond is a brilliant stone,
To catch the world's desire;
An opal holds a fiery spark;
But a flint holds fire.

An End

Love, strong as Death, is dead.
Come, let us make his bed
Among the dying flowers:
A green turf at his head;
And a stone at his feet,
Whereon we may sit
In the quiet evening hours.
He was born in the Spring,
And died before the harvesting:
On the last warm summer day
He left us; he would not stay
For Autumn twilight cold and grey.
Sit we by his grave, and sing
He is gone away.
To few chords and sad and low
Sing we so:
Be our eyes fixed on the grass
Shadow-veiled as the years pass
While we think of all that was
In the long ago.

An October Garden

In my Autumn garden I was fain
To mourn among my scattered roses;
Alas for that last rosebud which uncloses
To Autumn's languid sun and rain
When all the world is on the wane!
Which has not felt the sweet constraint of June,
Nor heard the nightingale in tune.
Broad-faced asters by my garden walk,
You are but coarse compared with roses:
More choice, more dear that rosebud which uncloses
Faint-scented, pinched, upon its stalk,
That least and last which cold winds balk;
A rose it is though least and last of all,
A rose to me though at the fall.

Angels At The Foot
Angels at the foot,
And Angels at the head,
And like a curly little lamb
My pretty babe in bed.

Another Spring

If I might see another Spring
I'd not plant summer flowers and wait:
I'd have my crocuses at once
My leafless pink mezereons,
My chill-veined snow-drops, choicer yet
My white or azure violet,
Leaf-nested primrose; anything
To blow at once, not late.
If I might see another Spring
I'd listen to the daylight birds
That build their nests and pair and sing,
Nor wait for mateless nightingale;
I'd listen to the lusty herds,
The ewes with lambs as white as snow,
I'd find out music in the hail
And all the winds that blow.
If I might see another Spring -
Oh stinging comment on my past
That all my past results in 'if' -
If I might see another Spring
I'd laugh today, today is brief
I would not wait for anything:
I'd use today that cannot last,
Be glad today and sing.

At Home

When I was dead, my spirit turned
To seek the much-frequented house:
I passed the door, and saw my friends
Feasting beneath green orange boughs;
From hand to hand they pushed the wine,
They sucked the pulp of plum and peach;
They sang, they jested, and they laughed,
For each was loved of each.
I listened to thier honest chat:
Said one: "To-morrow we shall be
Plod plod along the featureless sands,
And coasting miles and miles of sea."
Said one: "Before the turn of tide
We will achieve the eyrie-seat."
Said one: "To-morrow shall be like
To-day, but much more sweet."
"To-morrow," said they, strong with hope,
And dwelt upon the pleasant way:
"To-morrow," cried they, one and all,
While no one spoke of yesterday.
Their life stood full at blessed noon;
I, only I, had passed away:
"To-morrow and to-day," they cried;
I was of yesterday.
I shivered comfortless, but cast
No chill across the table-cloth;
I, all-forgotten, shivered, sad
To stay, and yet to part how loth:
I passed from the familiar room,
I who from love had passed away,
Like the remembrance of a guest
That tarrieth but a day.

Autumn

I dwell alone - I dwell alone, alone,
Whilst full my river flows down to the sea,
Gilded with flashing boats
That bring no friend to me:
O love-songs, gurgling from a hundred throats,
O love-pangs, let me be.
Fair fall the freighted boats which gold and stone
And spices bear to sea:
Slim, gleaming maidens swell their mellow notes,
Love-promising, entreating -
Ah! sweet, but fleeting -
Beneath the shivering, snow-white sails.
Hush! the wind flags and fails -
Hush! they will lie becalmed in sight of strand -
Sight of my strand, where I do dwell alone;
Their songs wake singing echoes in my land -
They cannot hear me moan.
One latest, solitary swallow flies
Across the sea, rough autumn-tempest tossed,
Poor bird, shall it be lost?
Dropped down into this uncongenial sea,
With no kind eyes
To watch it while it dies,
Unguessed, uncared for, free:
Set free at last,
The short pang past,
In sleep, in death, in dreamless sleep locked fast.
Mine avenue is all a growth of oaks,
Some rent by thunder strokes,
Some rustling leaves and acorns in the breeze;
Fair fall my fertile trees,
That rear their goodly heads, and live at ease.
A spider's web blocks all mine avenue;

He catches down and foolish painted flies,
That spider wary and wise.
Each morn it hangs a rainbow strung with dew
Betwixt boughs green with sap,
So fair, few creatures guess it is a trap:
I will not mar the web,
Though sad I am to see the small lives ebb.
It shakes - my trees shake - for a wind is roused
In cavern where it housed:
Each white and quivering sail,
Of boats among the water leaves
Hollows and strains in the full-throated gale:
Each maiden sings again -
Each languid maiden, whom the calm
Had lulled to sleep with rest and spice and balm
Miles down my river to the sea
They float and wane,
Long miles away from me.
Perhaps they say: 'She grieves,
Uplifted, like a beacon, on her tower.'
Perhaps they say: 'One hour
More, and we dance among the golden sheaves.'
Perhaps they say: 'One hour
More, and we stand,
Face to face, hand in hand;
Make haste, O slack gale, to the looked-for land!'
My trees are not in flower,
I have no bower,
And gusty creaks my tower,
And lonesome, very lonesome, is my strand.

Autumn Violets

Keep love for youth, and violets for the spring:
Of if these bloom when worn-out autumn grieves,
Let them lie hid in double shade of leaves,
Their own, and others dropped down withering;
For violets suit when home birds build and sing,
Not when the outbound bird a passage cleaves;
Not with dry stubble of mown harvest sheaves,
But when the green world buds to blossoming.
Keep violets for the spring, and love for youth,
Love that should dwell with beauty, mirth, and hope:
Or if a later sadder love be born,
Let this not look for grace beyond its scope,
But give itself, nor plead for answering truth—
A grateful Ruth tho' gleaning scanty corn.

Baby Cry

Baby cry -
Oh fie! -
At the physic in the cup:
Gulp it twice
And gulp it thrice,
Baby gulp it up.

Baby Lies So Fast Asleep
Baby lies so fast asleep
That we cannot wake her:
Will the angels clad in white
Fly from heaven to take her?
Baby lies so fast asleep
That no pain can grieve her;
Put a snowdrop in her hand,
Kiss her once and leave her.

Beauty Is Vain

While roses are so red,
While lilies are so white,
Shall a woman exalt her face
Because it gives delight?
She's not so sweet as a rose,
A lily's straighter than she,
And if she were as red or white
She'd be but one of three.
Whether she flush in love's summer
Or in its winter grow pale,
Whether she flaunt her beauty
Or hide it away in a veil,
Be she red or white,
And stand she erect or bowed,
Time will win the race he runs with her
And hide her away in a shroud.

Before The Paling Of The Stars

Before the winter morn,
Before the earliest cock crow,
Jesus Christ was born:
Born in a stable,
Cradled in a manger,
In the world his hands had made
Born a stranger.
Priest and king lay fast asleep
In Jerusalem;
Young and old lay fast asleep
In crowded Bethlehem;
Saint and angel, ox and ass,
Kept a watch together
Before the Christmas daybreak
In the winter weather.
Jesus on his mother's breast
In the stable cold,
Spotless lamb of God was he,
Shepherd of the fold:
Let us kneel with Mary maid,
With Joseph bent and hoary,
With saint and angel, ox and ass,
To hail the King of Glory.

Beneath Thy Cross

Am I a stone, and not a sheep,
That I can stand, O Christ, beneath thy cross,
To number drop by drop Thy Blood's slow loss,
And yet not weep?
Not so those women loved
Who with exceeding grief lamented Thee;
Not so fallen Peter weeping bitterly;
Not so the thief was moved;
Not so the Sun and Moon
Which hid their faces in a starless sky,
A horror of great darkness at broad noon--
I, only I.
Yet give not o'er,
But seek Thy sheep, true Shepherd of the flock;
Greater than Moses, turn and look once more
And smite a rock.

Bird Or Beast?

Did any bird come flying
After Adam and Eve,
When the door was shut against them
And they sat down to grieve?
I think not Eve's peacock
Splendid to see,
And I think not Adam's eagle;
But a dove may be.
Did any beast come pushing
Through the thorny hedge
Into the thorny thistly world,
Out from Eden's edge?
I think not a lion,
Though his strength is such;
But an innocent loving lamb
May have done as much.
If the dove preached from her bough
and the lamb from his sod,
The lamb and dove
Were preachers sent from God.

Bird Raptures

The sunrise wakes the lark to sing,
The moonrise wakes the nightingale.
Come darkness, moonrise, everything
That is so silent, sweet, and pale,
Come, so ye wake the nightingale.
Make haste to mount, thou wistful moon,
Make haste to wake the nightingale:
Let silence set the world in tune
To hearken to that wordless tale
Which warbles from the nightingale.
O herald skylark, stay thy flight
One moment, for a nightingale
Floods us with sorrow and delight.
To-morrow thou shalt hoist the sail;
Leave us tonight the nightingale.

Bitter For Sweet

Summer is gone with all its roses,
Its sun and perfumes and sweet flowers,
Its warm air and refreshing showers:
And even Autumn closes.
Yea, Autumn's chilly self is going,
And winter comes which is yet colder;
Each day the hoar-frost waxes bolder,
And the last buds cease blowing.

Blind From My Birth

Blind from my birth,
Where flowers are springing
I sit on earth
All dark.
Hark! hark!
A lark is singing.
His notes are all for me,
For me his mirth: -
Till some day I shall see
Beautiful flowers
And birds in bowers
Where all Joy Bells are ringing.

Boats Sail On The Rivers

Boats sail on the rivers,
And ships sail on the seas;
But clouds that sail across the sky
Are prettier far than these.
There are bridges on the rivers,
As pretty as you please;
But the bow that bridges heaven,
And overtops the trees,
And builds a road from earth to sky,
Is prettier far than these.

Bread And Milk For Breakfast
Bread and milk for breakfast,
And woollen frocks to wear,
And a crumb for robin redbreast
On the cold days of the year.

Bride Song

From 'The Prince's Progress'
TOO late for love, too late for joy,
Too late, too late!
You loiter'd on the road too long,
You trifled at the gate:
The enchanted dove upon her branch
Died without a mate;
The enchanted princess in her tower
Slept, died, behind the grate;
Her heart was starving all this while
You made it wait.
Ten years ago, five years ago,
One year ago,
Even then you had arrived in time,
Though somewhat slow;
Then you had known her living face
Which now you cannot know:
The frozen fountain would have leap'd,
The buds gone on to blow,
The warm south wind would have awaked
To melt the snow.
Is she fair now as she lies?
Once she was fair;
Meet queen for any kingly king,
With gold-dust on her hair.
Now there are poppies in her locks,
White poppies she must wear;
Must wear a veil to shroud her face
And the want graven there:
Or is the hunger fed at length,
Cast off the care?
We never saw her with a smile
Or with a frown;

Her bed seem'd never soft to her,
Though toss'd of down;

She little heeded what she wore,
Kirtle, or wreath, or gown;
We think her white brows often ached
Beneath her crown,
Till silvery hairs show'd in her locks
That used to be so brown.
We never heard her speak in haste:
Her tones were sweet,
And modulated just so much
As it was meet:
Her heart sat silent through the noise
And concourse of the street.
There was no hurry in her hands,
No hurry in her feet;
There was no bliss drew nigh to her,
That she might run to greet.
You should have wept her yesterday,
Wasting upon her bed:
But wherefore should you weep to-day
That she is dead?
Lo, we who love weep not to-day,
But crown her royal head.
Let be these poppies that we strew,
Your roses are too red:
Let be these poppies, not for you
Cut down and spread.

Brown And Furry

Brown and furry
Caterpillar in a hurry,
Take your walk
To the shady leaf, or stalk,
Or what not,
Which may be the chosen spot.
No toad spy you,
Hovering bird of prey pass by you;
Spin and die,
To live again a butterfly.

Brownie, Brownie, Let Down Your Milk
Brownie, Brownie, let down your milk
White as swansdown and smooth as silk,
Fresh as dew and pure as snow:
For I know where the cowslips blow,
And you shall have a cowslip wreath
No sweeter scented than your breath.

By The Sea

Why does the sea moan evermore?
Shut out from heaven it makes its moan,
It frets against the boundary shore;
All earth's full rivers cannot fill
The sea, that drinking thirsteth still.
Sheer miracles of loveliness
Lie hid in its unlooked-on bed:
Anemones, salt, passionless,
Blow flower-like; just enough alive
To blow and multiply and thrive.
Shells quaint with curve, or spot, or spike,
Encrusted live things argus-eyed,
All fair alike, yet all unlike,
Are born without a pang, and die
Without a pang, and so pass by.

By The Waters Of Babylon

Here where I dwell I waste to skin and bone;
The curse is come upon me, and I waste
In penal torment powerless to atone.
The curse is come on me, which makes no haste
And doth not tarry, crushing both the proud
Hard man and him the sinner double-faced.
Look not upon me, for my soul is bowed
Within me, as my body in this mire;
My soul crawls dumb-struck, sore-bested and cowed.
As Sodom and Gomorrah scourged by fire,
As Jericho before God's trumpet-peal,
So we the elect ones perish in His ire.
Vainly we gird on sackcloth, vainly kneel
With famished faces toward Jerusalem:
His heart is shut against us not to feel,
His ears against our cry He shutteth them,
His hand He shorteneth that He will not save,
His law is loud against us to condemn:
And we, as unclean bodies in the grave
Inheriting corruption and the dark,
Are outcast from His presence which we crave.
Our Mercy hath departed from His Ark,
Our Glory hath departed from His rest,
Our Shield hath left us naked as a mark
Unto all pitiless eyes made manifest.
Our very Father hath forsaken us,
Our God hath cast us from Him: we oppressed
Unto our foes are even marvellous,
A hissing and a butt for pointing hands,
Whilst God Almighty hunts and grinds us thus;
For He hath scattered us in alien lands,
Our priests, our princes, our anointed king,

And bound us hand and foot with brazen bands.
Here while I sit my painful heart takes wing
Home to the home-land I must see no more,
Where milk and honey flow, where waters spring
And fail not, where I dwelt in days of yore
Under my fig-tree and my fruitful vine,
There where my parents dwelt at ease before:

Now strangers press the olives that are mine,
Reap all the corners of my harvest-field,
And make their fat hearts wanton with my wine;
To them my trees, to them my garden yield
Their sweets and spices and their tender green,
O'er them in noontide heat outspread their shield.
Yet these are they whose fathers had not been
Housed with my dogs, whom hip and thigh we smote
And with their blood washed their pollutions clean,
Purging the land which spewed them from its throat;
Their daughters took we for a pleasant prey,
Choice tender ones on whom the fathers doat.
Now they in turn have led our own away;
Our daughters and our sisters and our wives
Sore weeping as they weep who curse the day,
To live, remote from help, dishonoured lives,
Soothing their drunken masters with a song,
Or dancing in their golden tinkling gyves:
Accurst if they remember through the long
Estrangement of their exile, twice accursed
If they forget and join the accursed throng.
How doth my heart that is so wrung not burst
When I remember that my way was plain,
And that God's candle lit me at the first,
Whilst now I grope in darkness, grope in vain,
Desiring but to find Him Who is lost,
To find Him once again, but once again.
His wrath came on us to the uttermost,
His covenanted and most righteous wrath:

Yet this is He of Whom we made our boast,
Who lit the Fiery Pillar in our path,
Who swept the Red Sea dry before our feet,
Who in His jealousy smote kings, and hath
Sworn once to David: One shall fill thy seat
Born of thy body, as the sun and moon
'Stablished for aye in sovereignty complete.
O Lord, remember David, and that soon.
The Glory hath departed, Ichabod!
Yet now, before our sun grow dark at noon,
Before we come to nought beneath Thy rod,
Before we go down quick into the pit,
Remember us for good, O God, our God:—

Thy Name will I remember, praising it,
Though Thou forget me, though Thou hide Thy face,
And blot me from the Book which Thou hast writ;
Thy Name will I remember in my praise
And call to mind Thy faithfulness of old,
Though as a weaver Thou cut off my days,
And end me as a tale ends that is told.

Child's Talk In April

I wish you were a pleasant wren,
And I your small accepted mate;
How we'd look down on toilsome men!
We'd rise and go to bed at eight
Or it may be not quite so late.
Then you should see the nest I'd build,
The wondrous nest for you and me;
The outside rough perhaps, but filled
With wool and down; ah, you should see
The cosy nest that it would be.
We'd have our change of hope and fear,
Small quarrels, reconcilements sweet:
I'd perch by you to chirp and cheer,
Or hop about on active feet,
And fetch you dainty bits to eat.
We'd be so happy by the day,
So safe and happy through the night,
We both should feel, and I should say,
It's all one season of delight,
And we'll make merry whilst we may,
Perhaps some day there'd be an egg
When spring had blossomed from the snow:
I'd stand triumphant on one leg;
Like chanticleer I'd almost crow
To let our little neighbours know.
Next you should sit and I would sing
Through lengthening days of sunny spring;
Till, if you wearied of the task,
I'd sit; and you should spread your wing

From bough to bough; I'd sit and bask.
Fancy the breaking of the shell,
The chirp, the chickens wet and bare,

The untried proud paternal swell;
And you with housewife-matron air
Enacting choicer bills of fare.
Fancy the embryo coats of down,
The gradual feathers soft and sleek;
Till clothed and strong from tail to crown,
With virgin warblings in their beak,
They too go forth to soar and seek.
So would it last an April through
And early summer fresh with dew,
Then should we part and live as twain:
Love-time would bring me back to you
And build our happy nest again.

Christian And Jew

A Dialogue
'Oh happy happy land!
Angels like rushes stand
About the wells of light.'—
'Alas, I have not eyes for this fair sight:
Hold fast my hand.'—
'As in a soft wind, they
Bend all one blessed way,
Each bowed in his own glory, star with star.'—
'I cannot see so far,
Here shadows are.'—
'White-winged the cherubim,
Yet whiter seraphim,
Glow white with intense fire of love.'—
'Mine eyes are dim:
I look in vain above,
And miss their hymn.'—
'Angels, Archangels cry
One to other ceaselessly
(I hear them sing)
One 'Holy, Holy, Holy' to their King.'—
'I do not hear them, I.'—
'At one side Paradise
Is curtained from the rest,
Made green for wearied eyes;
Much softer than the breast
Of mother-dove clad in a rainbow's dyes.
'All precious souls are there
Most safe, elect by grace,
All tears are wiped for ever from their face:
Untired in prayer
They wait and praise
Hidden for a little space.

'Boughs of the Living Vine
They spread in summer shine
Green leaf with leaf:
Sap of the Royal Vine it stirs like wine
In all both less and chief.
'Sing to the Lord,
All spirits of all flesh, sing;
For He hath not abhorred
Our low estate nor scorn'd our offering:
Shout to our King.'—
'But Zion said:
My Lord forgetteth me.
Lo, she hath made her bed
In dust; forsaken weepeth she
Where alien rivers swell the sea.
'She laid her body as the ground,
Her tender body as the ground to those
Who passed; her harpstrings cannot sound
In a strange land; discrowned
She sits, and drunk with woes.'—
'O drunken not with wine,
Whose sins and sorrows have fulfilled the sum,—
Be not afraid, arise, be no more dumb;
Arise, shine,
For thy light is come.'—
'Can these bones live?'—
'God knows:
The prophet saw such clothed with flesh and skin;
A wind blew on them and life entered in;
They shook and rose.
Hasten the time, O Lord, blot out their sin,
Let life begin.'

Christmas Eve

CHRISTMAS hath darkness
Brighter than the blazing noon,
Christmas hath a chillness
Warmer than the heat of June,
Christmas hath a beauty
Lovelier than the world can show:
For Christmas bringeth Jesus,
Brought for us so low.
Earth, strike up your music,
Birds that sing and bells that ring;
Heaven hath answering music
For all Angels soon to sing:
Earth, put on your whitest
Bridal robe of spotless snow:
For Christmas bringeth Jesus,
Brought for us so low.

Clever Little Willie Wee
Clever little Willie wee,
Bright-eyed, blue-eyed little fellow;
Merry little Margery
With her hair all yellow.
Little Willie in his heart
Is a sailor on the sea,
And he often cons a chart
With sister Margery.

Clouds

White sheep, white sheep,
On a blue hill,
When the wind stops,
You all stand still.
When the wind blows,
You walk away slow.
White sheep, white sheep,
Where do you go?

Cobwebs

It is a land with neither night nor day,
Nor heat nor cold, nor any wind, nor rain,
Nor hills nor valleys; but one even plain
Stretches thro' long unbroken miles away:
While thro' the sluggish air a twilight grey
Broodeth; no moons or seasons wax and wane,
No ebb and flow are there among the main,
No bud-time no leaf-falling there for aye,
No ripple on the sea, no shifting sand,
No beat of wings to stir the stagnant space,
And loveless sea: no trace of days before,
No guarded home, no time-worn restingplace
No future hope no fear forevermore.

Color

What is pink? a rose is pink
By a fountain's brink.
What is red? a poppy's red
In its barley bed.
What is blue? the sky is blue
Where the clouds float thro'.
What is white? a swan is white
Sailing in the light.
What is yellow? pears are yellow,
Rich and ripe and mellow.
What is green? the grass is green,
With small flowers between.
What is violet? clouds are violet
In the summer twilight.
What is orange? Why, an orange,
Just an orange!

Come Unto Me

Oh, for the time gone by, when thought of Christ
Made His Yoke easy and His Burden light;
When my heart stirred within me at the sight
Of Altar spread for awful Eucharist;
When all my hopes His promises sufficed,
When my Soul watched for Him by day, by night,
When my lamp lightened and my robe was white,
And all seemed loss, except the Pearl unpriced.
Yet, since He calls me still with tender Call,
Since He remembers Whom I half forgot,
I even will run my race and bear my lot:
For Faith the walls of Jericho cast down,
And Hope to whoso runs holds forth a Crown,
And Love is Christ, and Christ is All in all.

Conference Between Christ, The Saints, And The Soul

I am pale with sick desire,
For my heart is far away
From this world's fitful fire
And this world's waning day;
In a dream it overleaps
A world of tedious ills
To where the sunshine sleeps
On th' everlasting hills.
Say the Saints—There Angels ease us
Glorified and white.
They say—We rest in Jesus,
Where is not day nor night.
My Soul saith—I have sought
For a home that is not gained,
I have spent yet nothing bought,
Have laboured but not attained;
My pride strove to rise and grow,
And hath but dwindled down;
My love sought love, and lo!
Hath not attained its crown.
Say the Saints—Fresh Souls increase us,
None languish nor recede.
They say—We love our Jesus,
And He loves us indeed.
I cannot rise above,
I cannot rest beneath,
I cannot find out Love,
Nor escape from Death;
Dear hopes and joys gone by
Still mock me with a name;
My best beloved die
And I cannot die with them.

Say the Saints—No deaths decrease us,
Where our rest is glorious.
They say—We live in Jesus,
Who once died for us.

Oh, my Soul, she beats her wings
And pants to fly away
Up to immortal Things
In the Heavenly day:
Yet she flags and almost faints;
Can such be meant for me?
Come and see—say the Saints.
Saith Jesus—Come and see.
Say the Saints—His Pleasures please us
Before God and the Lamb.
Come and taste My Sweets—saith Jesus—
Be with Me where I am.

Consider

Consider
The lilies of the field whose bloom is brief:—
We are as they;
Like them we fade away,
As doth a leaf.
Consider
The sparrows of the air of small account:
Our God doth view
Whether they fall or mount,—
He guards us too.
Consider
The lilies that do neither spin nor toil,
Yet are most fair:—
What profits all this care
And all this coil?
Consider
The birds that have no barn nor harvest-weeks;
God gives them food:—
Much more our Father seeks
To do us good.
Helen Grey
Because one loves you, Helen Grey,
Is that a reason you should pout,
And like a March wind veer about,
And frown, and say your shrewish say?
Don't strain the cord until it snaps,
Don't split the sound heart with your wedge,
Don't cut your fingers with the edge
Of your keen wit; you may, perhaps.
Because you're handsome, Helen Grey,
Is that a reason to be proud?

Your eyes are bold, your laugh is loud,

Your steps go mincing on their way;
But so you miss that modest charm
Which is the surest charm of all:
Take heed, you yet may trip and fall,
And no man care to stretch his arm.
Stoop from your cold height, Helen Grey,
Come down, and take a lowlier place;
Come down, to fill it now with grace;
Come down you must perforce some day:
For years cannot be kept at bay,
And fading years will make you old;
Then in their turn will men seem cold,
When you yourself are nipped and grey.

Consider The Lilies Of The Field

Flowers preach to us if we will hear:—
The rose saith in the dewy morn:
I am most fair;
Yet all my loveliness is born
Upon a thorn.
The poppy saith amid the corn:
Let but my scarlet head appear
And I am held in scorn;
Yet juice of subtle virtue lies
Within my cup of curious dyes.
The lilies say: Behold how we
Preach without words of purity.
The violets whisper from the shade
Which their own leaves have made:
Men scent our fragrance on the air,
Yet take no heed
Of humble lessons we would read.
But not alone the fairest flowers:
The merest grass
Along the roadside where we pass,
Lichen and moss and sturdy weed,
Tell of His love who sends the dew,
The rain and sunshine too,
To nourish one small seed.

Cousin Kate

I was a cottage maiden
Hardened by sun and air
Contented with my cottage mates,
Not mindful I was fair.
Why did a great lord find me out,
And praise my flaxen hair?
Why did a great lord find me out,
To fill my heart with care?
He lured me to his palace home -
Woe's me for joy thereof-
To lead a shameless shameful life,
His plaything and his love.
He wore me like a silken knot,
He changed me like a glove;
So now I moan, an unclean thing,
Who might have been a dove.
O Lady kate, my cousin Kate,
You grew more fair than I:
He saw you at your father's gate,
Chose you, and cast me by.
He watched your steps along the lane,
Your work among the rye;
He lifted you from mean estate
To sit with him on high.
Because you were so good and pure
He bound you with his ring:
The neighbors call you good and pure,
Call me an outcast thing.
Even so I sit and howl in dust,
You sit in gold and sing:
Now which of us has tenderer heart?
You had the stronger wing.
O cousin Kate, my love was true,

Your love was writ in sand:
If he had fooled not me but you,

If you stood where I stand,
He'd not have won me with his love
Nor bought me with his land;
I would have spit into his face
And not have taken his hand.
Yet I've a gift you have not got,
And seem not like to get:
For all your clothes and wedding-ring
I've little doubt you fret.
My fair-haired son, my shame, my pride,
Cling closer, closer yet:
Your father would give his lands for one
To wear his coronet.

Crimson Curtains Round My Mother's Bed

Crimson curtains round my mother's bed,
Silken soft as may be;
Cool white curtains round about my bed,
For I am but a baby.

Crying, My Little One, Footsore And Weary?

Crying, my little one, footsore and weary?
Fall asleep, pretty one, warm on my shoulder:
I must tramp on through the winter night dreary,
While the snow falls on me colder and colder.
You are my one, and I have not another;
Sleep soft, my darling, my trouble and treasure;
Sleep warm and soft in the arms of your mother,
Dreaming of pretty things, dreaming of pleasure.

Currants On A Bush

Currants on a bush,
And figs upon a stem,
And cherries on a bending bough,
And Ned to gather them.

Dancing On The Hill-Tops

Dancing on the hill-tops,
Singing in the valleys,
Laughing with the echoes,
Merry little Alice.
Playing games with lambkins
In the flowering valleys,
Gathering pretty posies,
Helpful little Alice.
If her father's cottage
Turned into a palace,
And he owned the hill-tops
And the flowering valleys,
She'd be none the happier,
Happy little Alice.

De Profundis

Oh why is heaven built so far,
Oh why is earth set so remote?
I cannot reach the nearest star
That hangs afloat.
I would not care to reach the moon,
One round monotonous of change;
Yet even she repeats her tune
Beyond my range.
I never watch the scatter'd fire
Of stars, or sun's far-trailing train,
But all my heart is one desire,
And all in vain:
For I am bound with fleshly bands,
Joy, beauty, lie beyond my scope;
I strain my heart, I stretch my hands,
And catch at hope.

Dead Before Death

Ah! changed and cold, how changed and very cold,
With stiffened smiling lips and cold calm eyes:
Changed, yet the same; much knowing, little wise;
This was the promise of the days of old!
Grown hard and stubborn in the ancient mould,
Grown rigid in the sham of lifelong lies:
We hoped for better things as years would rise,
But it is over as a tale once told.
All fallen the blossom that no fruitage bore,
All lost the present and the future time,
All lost, all lost, the lapse that went before:
So lost till death shut-to the opened door,
So lost from chime to everlasting chime,
So cold and lost for ever evermore.

Dead Hope

Hope new born one pleasant morn
Died at even;
Hope dead lives nevermore.
No, not in heaven.
If his shroud were but a cloud
To weep itself away;
Or were he buried underground
To sprout some day!
But dead and gone is dead and gone
Vainly wept upon.
Nought we place above his face
To mark the spot,
But it shows a barren place
In our lot.
Hope has birth no more on earth
Morn or even;
Hope dead lives nevermore,
No, not in heaven.

Dead In The Cold, A Song-Singing Thrush

Dead in the cold, a song-singing thrush,
Dead at the foot of a snowberry bush, -
Weave him a coffin of rush,
Dig him a grave where the soft mosses grow,
Raise him a tombstone of snow.

Death's Chill Between

Chide not; let me breathe a little,
For I shall not mourn him long;
Though the life-cord was so brittle,
The love-cord was very strong.
I would wake a little space
Till I find a sleeping-place.
You can go,—I shall not weep;
You can go unto your rest.
My heart-ache is all too deep,
And too sore my throbbing breast.
Can sobs be, or angry tears,
Where are neither hopes nor fears?
Though with you I am alone
And must be so everywhere,
I will make no useless moan,—
None shall say 'She could not bear:'
While life lasts I will be strong,—
But I shall not struggle long.
Listen, listen! Everywhere
A low voice is calling me,
And a step is on the stair,
And one comes ye do not see,
Listen, listen! Evermore
A dim hand knocks at the door.
Hear me; he is come again,—
My own dearest is come back.
Bring him in from the cold rain;
Bring wine, and let nothing lack.
Thou and I will rest together,
Love, until the sunny weather.
I will shelter thee from harm,—
Hide thee from all heaviness.
Come to me, and keep thee warm

By my side in quietness.

I will lull thee to thy sleep
With sweet songs:—we will not weep.
Who hath talked of weeping?—Yet
There is something at my heart,
Gnawing, I would fain forget,
And an aching and a smart.
—Ah! my mother, 'tis in vain,
For he is not come again.

Despised And Rejected

My sun has set, I dwell
In darkness as a dead man out of sight;
And none remains, not one, that I should tell
To him mine evil plight
This bitter night.
I will make fast my door
That hollow friends may trouble me no more.
'Friend, open to Me.'—Who is this that calls?
Nay, I am deaf as are my walls:
Cease crying, for I will not hear
Thy cry of hope or fear.
Others were dear,
Others forsook me: what art thou indeed
That I should heed
Thy lamentable need?
Hungry should feed,
Or stranger lodge thee here?
'Friend, My Feet bleed.
Open thy door to Me and comfort Me.'
I will not open, trouble me no more.
Go on thy way footsore,
I will not rise and open unto thee.
'Then is it nothing to thee? Open, see
Who stands to plead with thee.
Open, lest I should pass thee by, and thou
One day entreat My Face
And howl for grace,
And I be deaf as thou art now.
Open to Me.'
Then I cried out upon him: Cease,
Leave me in peace:
Fear not that I should crave
Aught thou mayst have.

Leave me in peace, yea trouble me no more,
Lest I arise and chase thee from my door.

What, shall I not be let
Alone, that thou dost vex me yet?
But all night long that voice spake urgently:
'Open to Me.'
Still harping in mine ears:
'Rise, let Me in.'
Pleading with tears:
'Open to Me that I may come to thee.'
While the dew dropped, while the dark hours were cold:
'My Feet bleed, see My Face,
See My Hands bleed that bring thee grace,
My Heart doth bleed for thee,
Open to Me.'
So till the break of day:
Then died away
That voice, in silence as of sorrow;
Then footsteps echoing like a sigh
Passed me by,
Lingering footsteps slow to pass.
On the morrow
I saw upon the grass
Each footprint marked in blood, and on my door
The mark of blood for evermore.

Ding A Ding

'Ding a ding,'
The sweet bells sing,
And say:
'Come, all be gay'
For a wedding day.
'Dong a dong,'
The bells sigh long,
And call:
'Weep one, weep all'
For a funeral.

Dost Thou Not Care?
I love and love not: Lord, it breaks my heart
To love and not to love.
Thou veiled within Thy glory, gone apart
Into Thy shrine, which is above,
Dost Thou not love me, Lord, or care
For this mine ill?—
I love thee here or there,
I will accept thy broken heart, lie still.
Lord, it was well with me in time gone by
That cometh not again,
When I was fresh and cheerful, who but I?
I fresh, I cheerful: worn with pain
Now, out of sight and out of heart;
O Lord, how long?—
I watch thee as thou art,
I will accept thy fainting heart, be strong.
'Lie still,' 'be strong,' to-day; but, Lord, to-morrow,
What of to-morrow, Lord?
Shall there be rest from toil, be truce from sorrow,
Be living green upon the sward
Now but a barren grave to me,

Be joy for sorrow?—
Did I not die for thee?
Did I not live for thee? Leave Me to-morrow.

Dream Land

Where sunless rivers weep
Their waves into the deep,
She sleeps a charmed sleep:
Awake her not.
Led by a single star,
She came from very far
To seek where shadows are
Her pleasant lot.
She left the rosy morn,
She left the fields of corn,
For twilight cold and lorn
And water springs.
Through sleep, as through a veil,
She sees the sky look pale,
And hears the nightingale
That sadly sings.
Rest, rest, a perfect rest
Shed over brow and breast;
Her face is toward the west,
The purple land.
She cannot see the grain
Ripening on hill and plain;
She cannot feel the rain
Upon her hand.
Rest, rest, for evermore
Upon a mossy shore;
Rest, rest at the heart's core
Till time shall cease:
Sleep that no pain shall wake;
Night that no morn shall break
Till joy shall overtake
Her perfect peace.

Dream-Love

Young Love lies sleeping
In May-time of the year,
Among the lilies,
Lapped in the tender light:
White lambs come grazing,
White doves come building there:
And round about him
The May-bushes are white.
Soft moss the pillow
For oh, a softer cheek;
Broad leaves cast shadow
Upon the heavy eyes:
There winds and waters
Grow lulled and scarcely speak;
There twilight lingers
The longest in the skies.
Young Love lies dreaming;
But who shall tell the dream?
A perfect sunlight
On rustling forest tips;
Or perfect moonlight
Upon a rippling stream;
Or perfect silence,
Or song of cherished lips.
Burn odours round him
To fill the drowsy air;
Weave silent dances
Around him to and fro;
For oh, in waking
The sights are not so fair,
And song and silence
Are not like these below.
Young Love lies dreaming

Till summer days are gone,—
Dreaming and drowsing

Away to perfect sleep:

He sees the beauty
Sun hath not looked upon,
And tastes the fountain
Unutterably deep.
Him perfect music
Doth hush unto his rest,
And through the pauses
The perfect silence calms:
Oh, poor the voices
Of earth from east to west,
And poor earth's stillness
Between her stately palms.
Young Love lies drowsing
Away to poppied death;
Cool shadows deepen
Across the sleeping face:
So fails the summer
With warm, delicious breath;
And what hath autumn
To give us in its place?
Draw close the curtains
Of branched evergreen;
Change cannot touch them
With fading fingers sere:
Here the first violets
Perhaps will bud unseen,
And a dove, may be,
Return to nestle here.

Easter Even

There is nothing more that they can do
For all their rage and boast;
Caiaphas with his blaspheming crew,
Herod with his host,
Pontius Pilate in his Judgement-hall
Judging their Judge and his,
Or he who led them all and passed them all,
Arch-Judas with his kiss.
The sepulchre made sure with ponderous Stone,
Seal that same stone, O Priest;
It may be thou shalt block the holy One
From rising in the east:
Set a watch about the sepulchre
To watch on pain of death;
They must hold fast the stone if One should stir
And shake it from beneath.
God Almighty, He can break a seal
And roll away a Stone,
Can grind the proud in dust who would not kneel,
And crush the mighty one.
*
There is nothing more that they can do
For all their passionate care,
Those who sit in dust, the blessed few,
And weep and rend their hair:
Peter, Thomas, Mary Magdalene,

The Virgin unreproved,
Joseph, with Nicodemus, foremost men,
And John the Well-beloved,
Bring your finest linen and your spice,
Swathe the sacred Dead,
Bind with careful hands and piteous eyes

The napkin round His head;
Lay Him in the garden-rock to rest;
Rest you the Sabbath length:
The Sun that went down crimson in the west
Shall rise renewed in strength.
God Almighty shall give joy for pain,
Shall comfort him who grieves:
Lo! He with joy shall doubtless come again,
And with Him bring His sheaves.

Echo

Come to me in the silence of the night;
Come in the speaking silence of a dream;
Come with soft rounded cheeks and eyes as bright
As sunlight on a stream;
Come back in tears,
O memory, hope, love of finished years.
O dream how sweet, too sweet, too bitter sweet,
Whose wakening should have been in Paradise,
Where souls brimfull of love abide and meet;
Where thirsting longing eyes
Watch the slow door
That opening, letting in, lets out no more.
Yet come to me in dreams, that I may live
My very life again though cold in death:
Come back to me in dreams, that I may give
Pulse for pulse, breath for breath:
Speak low, lean low
As long ago, my love, how long ago.

Eight O'Clock

Eight o'clock;
The postman's knock!
Five letters for Papa;
One for Lou,
And none for you,
And three for dear Mamma.

Endure Hardness

A cold wind stirs the blackthorn
To burgeon and to blow,
Besprinkling half-green hedges
With flakes and sprays of snow.
Through coldness and through keenness,
Dear hearts, take comfort so:
Somewhere or other doubtless
These make the blackthorn blow.

Eve

'While I sit at the door
Sick to gaze within
Mine eye weepeth sore
For sorrow and sin:
As a tree my sin stands
To darken all lands;
Death is the fruit it bore.
'How have Eden bowers grown
Without Adam to bend them!
How have Eden flowers blown
Squandering their sweet breath
Without me to tend them!
The Tree of Life was ours,
Tree twelvefold-fruited,
Most lofty tree that flowers,
Most deeply rooted:
I chose the tree of death.
'Hadst thou but said me nay,
Adam, my brother,
I might have pined away;
I, but none other:
God might have let thee stay
Safe in our garden,
By putting me away
Beyond all pardon.
'I, Eve, sad mother
Of all who must live,
I, not another
Plucked bitterest fruit to give
My friend, husband, lover—
O wanton eyes, run over;
Who but I should grieve?—
Cain hath slain his brother:

Of all who must die mother,

Miserable Eve!'
Thus she sat weeping,
Thus Eve our mother,
Where one lay sleeping
Slain by his brother.
Greatest and least
Each piteous beast
To hear her voice
Forgot his joys
And set aside his feast.
The mouse paused in his walk
And dropped his wheaten stalk;
Grave cattle wagged their heads
In rumination;
The eagle gave a cry
From his cloud station;
Larks on thyme beds
Forbore to mount or sing;
Bees drooped upon the wing;
The raven perched on high
Forgot his ration;
The conies in their rock,
A feeble nation,
Quaked sympathetical;
The mocking-bird left off to mock;
Huge camels knelt as if
In deprecation;
The kind hart's tears were falling;
Chattered the wistful stork;
Dove-voices with a dying fall
Cooed desolation
Answering grief by grief.
Only the serpent in the dust
Wriggling and crawling,
Grinned an evil grin and thrust
His tongue out with its fork.

Fata Morgana

A blue-eyed phantom far before
Is laughing, leaping toward the sun:
Like lead I chase it evermore,
I pant and run.
It breaks the sunlight bound on bound:
Goes singing as it leaps along
To sheep-bells with a dreamy sound
A dreamy song.
I laugh, it is so brisk and gay;
It is so far before, I weep:
I hope I shall lie down some day,
Lie down and sleep.

Ferry Me Across The Water

'Ferry me across the water,
Do, boatman, do.'
'If you've a penny in your purse
I'll ferry you.'
'I have a penny in my purse,
And my eyes are blue;
So ferry me across the water,
Do, boatman, do.'
'Step into my ferry-boat,
Be they black or blue,
And for the penny in your purse
I'll ferry you.'

Fluttered Wings

The splendour of the kindling day,
The splendor of the setting sun,
These move my soul to wend its way,
And have done
With all we grasp and toil amongst and say.
The paling roses of a cloud,
The fading bow that arches space,
These woo my fancy toward my shroud,
Toward the place
Of faces veil'd, and heads discrown'd and bow'd.
The nation of the awful stars,
The wandering star whose blaze is brief,
These make me beat against the bars
Of my grief;
My tedious grief, twin to the life it mars.
O fretted heart toss'd to and fro,
So fain to flee, so fain to rest!
All glories that are high or low,
East or west,
Grow dim to thee who art so fain to go.

Fly Away, Fly Away Over The Sea

Fly away, fly away over the sea,
Sun-loving swallow, for summer is done;
Come again, come again, come back to me,
Bringing the summer and bringing the sun.

From "later Life"

VI

We lack, yet cannot fix upon the lack:
Not this, nor that; yet somewhat, certainly.
We see the things we do not yearn to see
Around us: and what see we glancing back?
Lost hopes that leave our hearts upon the rack,
Hopes that were never ours yet seem'd to be,
For which we steer'd on life's salt stormy sea
Braving the sunstroke and the frozen pack.
If thus to look behind is all in vain,
And all in vain to look to left or right,
Why face we not our future once again,
Launching with hardier hearts across the main,
Straining dim eyes to catch the invisible sight,
And strong to bear ourselves in patient pain?

IX

Star Sirius and the Pole Star dwell afar
Beyond the drawings each of other's strength:
One blazes through the brief bright summer's length
Lavishing life-heat from a flaming car;
While one unchangeable upon a throne
Broods o'er the frozen heart of earth alone,
Content to reign the bright particular star
Of some who wander or of some who groan.
They own no drawings each of other's strength,
Nor vibrate in a visible sympathy,
Nor veer along their courses each toward
Yet are their orbits pitch'd in harmony
Of one dear heaven, across whose depth and length
Mayhap they talk together without speech.

From House To House

The first was like a dream through summer heat,
The second like a tedious numbing swoon,
While the half-frozen pulses lagged to beat
Beneath a winter moon.
'But,' says my friend, 'what was this thing and where?'
It was a pleasure-place within my soul;
An earthly paradise supremely fair
That lured me from the goal.
The first part was a tissue of hugged lies;
The second was its ruin fraught with pain:
Why raise the fair delusion to the skies
But to be dashed again?
My castle stood of white transparent glass
Glittering and frail with many a fretted spire,
But when the summer sunset came to pass
It kindled into fire.
My pleasaunce was an undulating green,
Stately with trees whose shadows slept below,
With glimpses of smooth garden-beds between
Like flame or sky or snow.
Swift squirrels on the pastures took their ease,
With leaping lambs safe from the unfeared knife;
All singing-birds rejoicing in those trees
Fulfilled their careless life.
Woodpigeons cooed there, stockdoves nestled there;
My trees were full of songs and flowers and fruit,
Their branches spread a city to the air
And mice lodged in their root.
My heath lay farther off, where lizards lived
In strange metallic mail, just spied and gone;
Like darted lightnings here and there perceived
But nowhere dwelt upon.

Frogs and fat toads were there to hop or plod

And propagate in peace, an uncouth crew,
Where velvet-headed rushes rustling nod
And spill the morning dew.
All caterpillars throve beneath my rule,
With snails and slugs in corners out of sight;
I never marred the curious sudden stool
That perfects in a night.
Safe in his excavated gallery
The burrowing mole groped on from year to year;
No harmless hedgehog curled because of me
His prickly back for fear.
Oft times one like an angel walked with me,
With spirit-discerning eyes like flames of fire,
But deep as the unfathomed endless sea,
Fulfilling my desire:
And sometimes like a snowdrift he was fair,
And sometimes like a sunset glorious red,
And sometimes he had wings to scale the air
With aureole round his head.
We sang our songs together by the way,
Calls and recalls and echoes of delight;
So communed we together all the day,
And so in dreams by night.
I have no words to tell what way we walked.
What unforgotten path now closed and sealed;
I have no words to tell all things we talked,
All things that he revealed:
This only can I tell: that hour by hour
I waxed more feastful, lifted up and glad;
I felt no thorn-prick when I plucked a flower,
Felt not my friend was sad.
'To-morrow,' once I said to him with smiles:

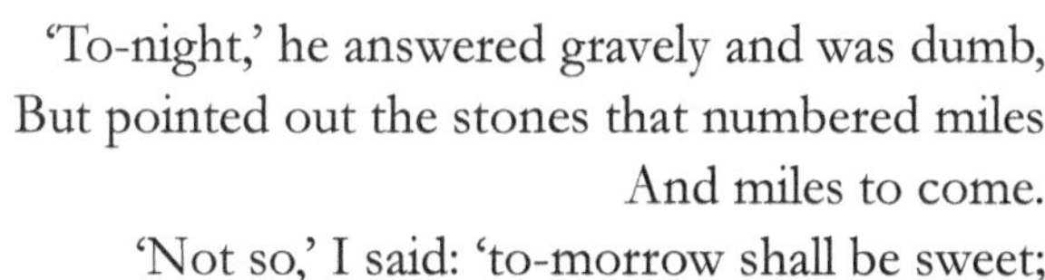

'To-night,' he answered gravely and was dumb,
But pointed out the stones that numbered miles
And miles to come.
'Not so,' I said: 'to-morrow shall be sweet;

To-night is not so sweet as coming days.'
Then first I saw that he had turned his feet,
Had turned from me his face:
Running and flying miles and miles he went,
But once looked back to beckon with his hand
And cry: 'Come home, O love, from banishment:
Come to the distant land.'
That night destroyed me like an avalanche;
One night turned all my summer back to snow:
Next morning not a bird upon my branch,
Not a lamb woke below,—
No bird, no lamb, no living breathing thing;
No squirrel scampered on my breezy lawn,
No mouse lodged by his hoard: all joys took wing
And fled before that dawn.
Azure and sun were starved from heaven above,
No dew had fallen, but biting frost lay hoar:
O love, I knew that I should meet my love,
Should find my love no more.
'My love no more,' I muttered stunned with pain:
I shed no tear, I wrung no passionate hand,
Till something whispered: 'You shall meet again,
Meet in a distant land.'
Then with a cry like famine I arose,
I lit my candle, searched from room to room,
Searched up and down; a war of winds that froze
Swept through the blank of gloom.
I searched day after day, night after night;
Scant change there came to me of night or day:
'No more,' I wailed, 'no more:' and trimmed my light,

And gnashed but did not pray,

Until my heart broke and my spirit broke:
Upon the frost-bound floor I stumbled, fell,
And moaned: 'It is enough: withhold the stroke.
Farewell, O love, farewell.'
Then life swooned from me. And I heard the song
Of spheres and spirits rejoicing over me:
One cried: 'Our sister, she hath suffered long.'—
One answered: 'Make her see.'—
One cried: 'Oh blessed she who no more pain,
Who no more disappointment shall receive.'—
One answered: 'Not so: she must live again;
Strengthen thou her to live.'
So while I lay entranced a curtain seemed
To shrivel with crackling from before my face;
Across mine eyes a waxing radiance beamed
And showed a certain place.
I saw a vision of a woman, where
Night and new morning strive for domination;
Incomparably pale, and almost fair,
And sad beyond expression.
Her eyes were like some fire-enshrining gem,
Were stately like the stars, and yet were tender;
Her figure charmed me like a windy stem
Quivering and drooped and slender.
I stood upon the outer barren ground,
She stood on inner ground that budded flowers;
While circling in their never-slackening round
Danced by the mystic hours.
But every flower was lifted on a thorn,
And every thorn shot upright from its sands
To gall her feet; hoarse laughter pealed in scorn
With cruel clapping hands.

She bled and wept, yet did not shrink; her strength
Was strung up until daybreak of delight:
She measured measureless sorrow toward its length,
And breadth, and depth, and height.
Then marked I how a chain sustained her form,
A chain of living links not made nor riven:
It stretched sheer up through lighting, wind, and storm,
And anchored fast in heaven.
One cried: 'How long? yet founded on the Rock
She shall do battle, suffer, and attain.'—
One answered: 'Faith quakes in the tempest shock:
Strengthen her soul again.'
I saw a cup sent down and come to her
Brimfull of loathing and of bitterness:
She drank with livid lips that seemed to stir
The depth, not make it less.
But as she drank I spied a hand distil
New wine and virgin honey; making it
First bitter-sweet, then sweet indeed, until
She tasted only sweet.
Her lips and cheeks waxed rosy-fresh and young;
Drinking she sang: 'My soul shall nothing want;'
And drank anew: while soft a song was sung,
A mystical slow chant.
One cried: 'The wounds are faithful of a friend:
The wilderness shall blossom as a rose.'—
One answered: 'Rend the veil, declare the end,
Strengthen her ere she goes.'
Then earth and heaven were rolled up like a scroll;
Time and space, change and death, had passed away;
Weight, number, measure, each had reached its whole;
The day had come, that day.
Multitudes—multitudes—stood up in bliss,
Made equal to the angels, glorious, fair;

With harps, palms, wedding-garments, kiss of peace,
And crowned and haloed hair.

They sang a song, a new song in the height,
Harping with harps to Him Who is Strong and True:
They drank new wine, their eyes saw with new light,
Lo, all things were made new.
Tier beyond tier they rose and rose and rose
So high that it was dreadful, flames with flames:
No man could number them, no tongue disclose
Their secret sacred names.
As though one pulse stirred all, one rush of blood
Fed all, one breath swept through them myriad-voiced,
They struck their harps, cast down their crowns, they stood
And worshipped and rejoiced.
Each face looked one way like a moon new-lit,
Each face looked one way towards its Sun of Love;
Drank love and bathed in love and mirrored it
And knew no end thereof.
Glory touched glory on each blessed head,
Hands locked dear hands never to sunder more:
These were the new-begotten from the dead
Whom the great birthday bore.
Heart answered heart, soul answered soul at rest,
Double against each other, filled, sufficed:
All loving, loved of all; but loving best
And best beloved of Christ.
I saw that one who lost her love in pain,
Who trod on thorns, who drank the loathsome cup;
The lost in night, in day was found again;
The fallen was lifted up.
They stood together in the blessed noon,
They sang together through the length of days;
Each loving face bent Sunwards like a moon
New-lit with love and praise.

Therefore, O friend, I would not if I might
Rebuild my house of lies, wherein I joyed
One time to dwell: my soul shall walk in white,
Cast down but not destroyed.

Therefore in patience I possess my soul;
Yea, therefore as a flint I set my face,
To pluck down, to build up again the whole—
But in a distant place.
These thorns are sharp, yet I can tread on them;
This cup is loathsome, yet He makes it sweet:
My face is steadfast toward Jerusalem,
My heart remembers it.
I lift the hanging hands, the feeble knees—
I, precious more than seven times molten gold—
Until the day when from his storehouses
God shall bring new and old;
Beauty for ashes, oil of joy for grief,
Garment of praise for spirit of heaviness:
Although to-day I fade as doth a leaf,
I languish and grow less.
Although to-day He prunes my twigs with pain,
Yet doth His blood nourish and warm my root:
To-morrow I shall put forth buds again
And clothe myself with fruit.
Although to-day I walk in tedious ways,
To-day His staff is turned into a rod,
Yet will I wait for Him the appointed days
And stay upon my God.

From Sunset To Star Rise

Go from me, summer friends, and tarry not:
I am no summer friend, but wintry cold,
A silly sheep benighted from the fold,
A sluggard with a thorn-choked garden plot.
Take counsel, sever from my lot your lot,
Dwell in your pleasant places, hoard your gold;
Lest you with me should shiver on the wold,
Athirst and hungering on a barren spot.
For I have hedged me with a thorny hedge,
I live alone, I look to die alone:
Yet sometimes, when a wind sighs through the sedge,
Ghosts of my buried years, and friends come back,
My heart goes sighing after swallows flown
On sometime summer's unreturning track.

From The Antique

It's a weary life, it is, she said:
Doubly blank in a woman's lot:
I wish and I wish I were a man:
Or, better then any being, were not:
Were nothing at all in all the world,
Not a body and not a soul:
Not so much as a grain of dust
Or a drop of water from pole to pole.
Still the world would wag on the same,
Still the seasons go and come:
Blossoms bloom as in days of old,
Cherries ripen and wild bees hum.
None would miss me in all the world,
How much less would care or weep:
I should be nothing, while all the rest
Would wake and weary and fall asleep.

Give Me Holly

But give me holly, bold and jolly,
Honest, prickly, shining holly;
Pluck me holly leaf and berry
For the day when I make merry

Goblin Market

MORNING and evening
Maids heard the goblins cry:
"Come buy our orchard fruits,
Come buy, come buy:
Apples and quinces,
Lemons and oranges,
Plump unpecked cherries-
Melons and raspberries,
Bloom-down-cheeked peaches,
Swart-headed mulberries,
Wild free-born cranberries,
Crab-apples, dewberries,
Pine-apples, blackberries,
Apricots, strawberries--
All ripe together
In summer weather--
Morns that pass by,
Fair eves that fly;
Come buy, come buy;
Our grapes fresh from the vine,
Pomegranates full and fine,
Dates and sharp bullaces,
Rare pears and greengages,
Damsons and bilberries,
Taste them and try:
Currants and gooseberries,
Bright-fire-like barberries,
Figs to fill your mouth,
Citrons from the South,
Sweet to tongue and sound to eye,

Come buy, come buy."
Evening by evening
Among the brookside rushes,
Laura bowed her head to hear,
Lizzie veiled her blushes:
Crouching close together
In the cooling weather,
With clasping arms and cautioning lips,

With tingling cheeks and finger-tips.
"Lie close," Laura said,
Pricking up her golden head:
We must not look at goblin men,
We must not buy their fruits:
Who knows upon what soil they fed
Their hungry thirsty roots?"
"Come buy," call the goblins
Hobbling down the glen.
"O! cried Lizzie, Laura, Laura,
You should not peep at goblin men."
Lizzie covered up her eyes
Covered close lest they should look;
Laura reared her glossy head,
And whispered like the restless brook:
"Look, Lizzie, look, Lizzie,
Down the glen tramp little men.
One hauls a basket,
One bears a plate,
One lugs a golden dish
Of many pounds' weight.
How fair the vine must grow
Whose grapes are so luscious;
How warm the wind must blow
Through those fruit bushes."
"No," said Lizzie, "no, no, no;

Their offers should not charm us,
Their evil gifts would harm us."
She thrust a dimpled finger
In each ear, shut eyes and ran:
Curious Laura chose to linger
Wondering at each merchant man.
One had a cat's face,
One whisked a tail,
One tramped at a rat's pace,
One crawled like a snail,
One like a wombat prowled obtuse and furry,
One like a ratel tumbled hurry-scurry.
Lizzie heard a voice like voice of doves
Cooing all together:
They sounded kind and full of loves
In the pleasant weather.

Laura stretched her gleaming neck
Like a rush-imbedded swan,
Like a lily from the beck,
Like a moonlit poplar branch,
Like a vessel at the launch
When its last restraint is gone.
Backwards up the mossy glen
Turned and trooped the goblin men,
With their shrill repeated cry,
"Come buy, come buy."
When they reached where Laura was
They stood stock still upon the moss,
Leering at each other,
Brother with queer brother;
Signalling each other,
Brother with sly brother.
One set his basket down,
One reared his plate;

One began to weave a crown
Of tendrils, leaves, and rough nuts brown
(Men sell not such in any town);
One heaved the golden weight
Of dish and fruit to offer her:
"Come buy, come buy," was still their cry.
Laura stared but did not stir,
Longed but had no money:
The whisk-tailed merchant bade her taste
In tones as smooth as honey,
The cat-faced purr'd,
The rat-paced spoke a word
Of welcome, and the snail-paced even was heard;
One parrot-voiced and jolly
Cried "Pretty Goblin" still for "Pretty Polly";
One whistled like a bird.
But sweet-tooth Laura spoke in haste:
"Good folk, I have no coin;
To take were to purloin:
I have no copper in my purse,
I have no silver either,

And all my gold is on the furze
That shakes in windy weather
Above the rusty heather."
"You have much gold upon your head,"
They answered altogether:
"Buy from us with a golden curl."
She clipped a precious golden lock,
She dropped a tear more rare than pearl,
Then sucked their fruit globes fair or red:
Sweeter than honey from the rock,
Stronger than man-rejoicing wine,
Clearer than water flowed that juice;
She never tasted such before,

How should it cloy with length of use?
She sucked and sucked and sucked the more
Fruits which that unknown orchard bore,
She sucked until her lips were sore;
Then flung the emptied rinds away,
But gathered up one kernel stone,
And knew not was it night or day
As she turned home alone.
Lizzie met her at the gate
Full of wise upbraidings:
"Dear, you should not stay so late,
Twilight is not good for maidens;
Should not loiter in the glen
In the haunts of goblin men.
Do you not remember Jeanie,
How she met them in the moonlight,
Took their gifts both choice and many,
Ate their fruits and wore their flowers
Plucked from bowers
Where summer ripens at all hours?
But ever in the moonlight
She pined and pined away;
Sought them by night and day,
Found them no more, but dwindled and grew gray;
Then fell with the first snow,
While to this day no grass will grow
Where she lies low:
I planted daisies there a year ago

That never blow.
You should not loiter so."
"Nay hush," said Laura.
"Nay hush, my sister:
I ate and ate my fill,
Yet my mouth waters still;

To-morrow night I will
Buy more," and kissed her.
"Have done with sorrow;
I'll bring you plums to-morrow
Fresh on their mother twigs,
Cherries worth getting;
You cannot think what figs
My teeth have met in,
What melons, icy-cold
Piled on a dish of gold
Too huge for me to hold,
What peaches with a velvet nap,
Pellucid grapes without one seed:
Odorous indeed must be the mead
Whereon they grow, and pure the wave they drink,
With lilies at the brink,
And sugar-sweet their sap."
Golden head by golden head,
Like two pigeons in one nest
Folded in each other's wings,
They lay down, in their curtained bed:
Like two blossoms on one stem,
Like two flakes of new-fallen snow,
Like two wands of ivory
Tipped with gold for awful kings.
Moon and stars beamed in at them,
Wind sang to them lullaby,
Lumbering owls forbore to fly,
Not a bat flapped to and fro
Round their rest:
Cheek to cheek and breast to breast
Locked together in one nest.
Early in the morning
When the first cock crowed his warning,
Neat like bees, as sweet and busy,
Laura rose with Lizzie:

Fetched in honey, milked the cows,
Aired and set to rights the house,
Kneaded cakes of whitest wheat,
Cakes for dainty mouths to eat,
Next churned butter, whipped up cream,
Fed their poultry, sat and sewed;
Talked as modest maidens should
Lizzie with an open heart,
Laura in an absent dream,
One content, one sick in part;
One warbling for the mere bright day's delight,
One longing for the night.
At length slow evening came--
They went with pitchers to the reedy brook;
Lizzie most placid in her look,
Laura most like a leaping flame.
They drew the gurgling water from its deep
Lizzie plucked purple and rich golden flags,
Then turning homeward said: "The sunset flushes
Those furthest loftiest crags;
Come, Laura, not another maiden lags,
No wilful squirrel wags,
The beasts and birds are fast asleep."
But Laura loitered still among the rushes
And said the bank was steep.
And said the hour was early still,
The dew not fallen, the wind not chill:
Listening ever, but not catching
The customary cry,
"Come buy, come buy,"
With its iterated jingle
Of sugar-baited words:
Not for all her watching
Once discerning even one goblin
Racing, whisking, tumbling, hobbling;

Let alone the herds
That used to tramp along the glen,
In groups or single,

Of brisk fruit-merchant men.
Till Lizzie urged, "O Laura, come,
I hear the fruit-call, but I dare not look:
You should not loiter longer at this brook:
Come with me home.
The stars rise, the moon bends her arc,
Each glow-worm winks her spark,
Let us get home before the night grows dark;
For clouds may gather even
Though this is summer weather,
Put out the lights and drench us through;
Then if we lost our way what should we do?"
Laura turned cold as stone
To find her sister heard that cry alone,
That goblin cry,
"Come buy our fruits, come buy."
Must she then buy no more such dainty fruit?
Must she no more such succous pasture find,
Gone deaf and blind?
Her tree of life drooped from the root:
She said not one word in her heart's sore ache;
But peering thro' the dimness, naught discerning,
Trudged home, her pitcher dripping all the way;
So crept to bed, and lay
Silent 'til Lizzie slept;
Then sat up in a passionate yearning,
And gnashed her teeth for balked desire, and wept
As if her heart would break.
Day after day, night after night,
Laura kept watch in vain,
In sullen silence of exceeding pain.

She never caught again the goblin cry:
"Come buy, come buy,"
She never spied the goblin men
Hawking their fruits along the glen:
But when the noon waxed bright
Her hair grew thin and gray;
She dwindled, as the fair full moon doth turn
To swift decay, and burn

Her fire away.
One day remembering her kernel-stone
She set it by a wall that faced the south;
Dewed it with tears, hoped for a root,
Watched for a waxing shoot,
But there came none;
It never saw the sun,
It never felt the trickling moisture run:
While with sunk eyes and faded mouth
She dreamed of melons, as a traveller sees
False waves in desert drouth
With shade of leaf-crowned trees,
And burns the thirstier in the sandful breeze.
She no more swept the house,
Tended the fowls or cows,
Fetched honey, kneaded cakes of wheat,
Brought water from the brook:
But sat down listless in the chimney-nook
And would not eat.
Tender Lizzie could not bear
To watch her sister's cankerous care,
Yet not to share.
She night and morning
Caught the goblins' cry:
"Come buy our orchard fruits,
Come buy, come buy."

Beside the brook, along the glen
She heard the tramp of goblin men,
The voice and stir
Poor Laura could not hear;
Longed to buy fruit to comfort her,
But feared to pay too dear.
She thought of Jeanie in her grave,
Who should have been a bride;
But who for joys brides hope to have
Fell sick and died
In her gay prime,
In earliest winter-time,

With the first glazing rime,
With the first snow-fall of crisp winter-time.
Till Laura, dwindling,
Seemed knocking at Death's door:
Then Lizzie weighed no more
Better and worse,
But put a silver penny in her purse,
Kissed Laura, crossed the heath with clumps of furze
At twilight, halted by the brook,
And for the first time in her life
Began to listen and look.
Laughed every goblin
When they spied her peeping:
Came towards her hobbling,
Flying, running, leaping,
Puffing and blowing,
Chuckling, clapping, crowing,
Clucking and gobbling,
Mopping and mowing,
Full of airs and graces,
Pulling wry faces,
Demure grimaces,

Cat-like and rat-like,
Ratel and wombat-like,
Snail-paced in a hurry,
Parrot-voiced and whistler,
Helter-skelter, hurry-skurry,
Chattering like magpies,
Fluttering like pigeons,
Gliding like fishes, --
Hugged her and kissed her;
Squeezed and caressed her;
Stretched up their dishes,
Panniers and plates:
"Look at our apples
Russet and dun,
Bob at our cherries
Bite at our peaches,
Citrons and dates,
Grapes for the asking,

Pears red with basking
Out in the sun,
Plums on their twigs;
Pluck them and suck them,
Pomegranates, figs."
"Good folk," said Lizzie,
Mindful of Jeanie,
"Give me much and many"; --
Held out her apron,
Tossed them her penny.
"Nay, take a seat with us,
Honor and eat with us,"
They answered grinning;
"Our feast is but beginning.
Night yet is early,
Warm and dew-pearly,

Wakeful and starry:
Such fruits as these
No man can carry;
Half their bloom would fly,
Half their dew would dry,
Half their flavor would pass by.
Sit down and feast with us,
Be welcome guest with us,
Cheer you and rest with us."
"Thank you," said Lizzie; "but one waits
At home alone for me:
So, without further parleying,
If you will not sell me any
Of your fruits though much and many,
Give me back my silver penny
I tossed you for a fee."
They began to scratch their pates,
No longer wagging, purring,
But visibly demurring,
Grunting and snarling.
One called her proud,
Cross-grained, uncivil;
Their tones waxed loud,
Their looks were evil.
Lashing their tails

They trod and hustled her,
Elbowed and jostled her,
Clawed with their nails,
Barking, mewing, hissing, mocking,
Tore her gown and soiled her stocking,
Twitched her hair out by the roots,
Stamped upon her tender feet,
Held her hands and squeezed their fruits
Against her mouth to make her eat.

White and golden Lizzie stood,
Like a lily in a flood,
Like a rock of blue-veined stone
Lashed by tides obstreperously, --
Like a beacon left alone
In a hoary roaring sea,
Sending up a golden fire, --
Like a fruit-crowned orange-tree
White with blossoms honey-sweet
Sore beset by wasp and bee, --
Like a royal virgin town
Topped with gilded dome and spire
Close beleaguered by a fleet
Mad to tear her standard down.
One may lead a horse to water,
Twenty cannot make him drink.
Though the goblins cuffed and caught her,
Coaxed and fought her,
Bullied and besought her,
Scratched her, pinched her black as ink,
Kicked and knocked her,
Mauled and mocked her,
Lizzie uttered not a word;
Would not open lip from lip
Lest they should cram a mouthful in;
But laughed in heart to feel the drip
Of juice that syruped all her face,
And lodged in dimples of her chin,
And streaked her neck which quaked like curd.
At last the evil people,
Worn out by her resistance,

Flung back her penny, kicked their fruit
Along whichever road they took,
Not leaving root or stone or shoot.

Some writhed into the ground,
Some dived into the brook
With ring and ripple.
Some scudded on the gale without a sound,
Some vanished in the distance.
In a smart, ache, tingle,
Lizzie went her way;
Knew not was it night or day;
Sprang up the bank, tore through the furze,
Threaded copse and dingle,
And heard her penny jingle
Bouncing in her purse, --
Its bounce was music to her ear.
She ran and ran
As if she feared some goblin man
Dogged her with gibe or curse
Or something worse:
But not one goblin skurried after,
Nor was she pricked by fear;
The kind heart made her windy-paced
That urged her home quite out of breath with haste
And inward laughter.
She cried "Laura," up the garden,
"Did you miss me ?
Come and kiss me.
Never mind my bruises,
Hug me, kiss me, suck my juices
Squeezed from goblin fruits for you,
Goblin pulp and goblin dew.
Eat me, drink me, love me;
Laura, make much of me:
For your sake I have braved the glen
And had to do with goblin merchant men."
Laura started from her chair,
Flung her arms up in the air,

Clutched her hair:

"Lizzie, Lizzie, have you tasted
For my sake the fruit forbidden?
Must your light like mine be hidden,
Your young life like mine be wasted,
Undone in mine undoing,
And ruined in my ruin;
Thirsty, cankered, goblin-ridden?"
She clung about her sister,
Kissed and kissed and kissed her:
Tears once again
Refreshed her shrunken eyes,
Dropping like rain
After long sultry drouth;
Shaking with aguish fear, and pain,
She kissed and kissed her with a hungry mouth.
Her lips began to scorch,
That juice was wormwood to her tongue,
She loathed the feast:
Writhing as one possessed she leaped and sung,
Rent all her robe, and wrung
Her hands in lamentable haste,
And beat her breast.
Her locks streamed like the torch
Borne by a racer at full speed,
Or like the mane of horses in their flight,
Or like an eagle when she stems the light
Straight toward the sun,
Or like a caged thing freed,
Or like a flying flag when armies run.
Swift fire spread through her veins, knocked
at her heart,
Met the fire smouldering there
And overbore its lesser flame,

She gorged on bitterness without a name:
Ah! fool, to choose such part
Of soul-consuming care!
Sense failed in the mortal strife:
Like the watch-tower of a town
Which an earthquake shatters down,
Like a lightning-stricken mast,
Like a wind-uprooted tree

Spun about,
Like a foam-topped water-spout
Cast down headlong in the sea,
She fell at last;
Pleasure past and anguish past,
Is it death or is it life ?
Life out of death.
That night long Lizzie watched by her,
Counted her pulse's flagging stir,
Felt for her breath,
Held water to her lips, and cooled her face
With tears and fanning leaves:
But when the first birds chirped about their eaves,
And early reapers plodded to the place
Of golden sheaves,
And dew-wet grass
Bowed in the morning winds so brisk to pass,
And new buds with new day
Opened of cup-like lilies on the stream,
Laura awoke as from a dream,
Laughed in the innocent old way,
Hugged Lizzie but not twice or thrice;
Her gleaming locks showed not one thread of gray,
Her breath was sweet as May,
And light danced in her eyes.
Days, weeks, months,years

Afterwards, when both were wives
With children of their own;
Their mother-hearts beset with fears,
Their lives bound up in tender lives;
Laura would call the little ones
And tell them of her early prime,
Those pleasant days long gone
Of not-returning time:
Would talk about the haunted glen,
The wicked, quaint fruit-merchant men,
Their fruits like honey to the throat,
But poison in the blood;
(Men sell not such in any town;)
Would tell them how her sister stood

In deadly peril to do her good,
And win the fiery antidote:
Then joining hands to little hands
Would bid them cling together,
"For there is no friend like a sister,
In calm or stormy weather,
To cheer one on the tedious way,
To fetch one if one goes astray,
To lift one if one totters down,
To strengthen whilst one stands."

Gone For Ever

O happy rosebud blooming
Upon thy parent tree,
Nay, thou art too presuming
For soon the earth entombing
Thy faded charms shall be,
And the chill damp consuming.
O happy skylark springing
Up to the broad blue sky,
Too fearless in thy winging,
Too gladsome in thy singing,
Thou also soon shalt lie
Where no sweet notes are ringing.
And through life's shine and shower
We shall have joy and pain;
But in the summer bower,
And at the morning hour,
We still shall look in vain
For the same bird and flower.

Good Friday

Am I a stone and not a sheep
That I can stand, O Christ, beneath Thy Cross,
To number drop by drop Thy Blood's slow loss,
And yet not weep?
Not so those women loved
Who with exceeding grief lamented Thee;
Not so fallen Peter weeping bitterly;
Not so the thief was moved;
Not so the Sun and Moon
Which hid their faces in a starless sky,
A horror of great darkness at broad noon—
I, only I.
Yet give not o'er,
But seek Thy sheep, true Shepherd of the flock;
Greater than Moses, turn and look once more
And smite a rock.

Goodbye In Fear, Goodbye In Sorrow,

'Goodbye in fear, goodbye in sorrow,
Goodbye, and all in vain,
Never to meet again, my dear -'
'Never to part again.'
'Goodbye today, goodbye tomorrow,
Goodbye till earth shall wane,
Never to meet again, my dear -'
'Never to part again.'

Growing In The Vale

Growing in the vale
By the uplands hilly,
Growing straight and frail,
Lady Daffadowndilly.
In a golden crown,
And a scant green gown
While the spring blows chilly,
Lady Daffadown,
Sweet Daffadowndilly.

Grown And Flown

I loved my love from green of Spring
Until sere Autumn's fall;
But now that leaves are withering
How should one love at all?
One heart's too small
For hunger, cold, love, everything.
I loved my love on sunny days
Until late Summer's wane;
But now that frost begins to glaze
How should one love again ?
Nay, love and pain
Walk wide apart in diverse ways.
I loved my love - alas to see
That this should be, alas!
I thought that this could scarcely be,
Yet has it come to pass:
Sweet sweet love was,
Now bitter bitter grown to me.

Hear What The Mournful Linnets Say

Hear what the mournful linnets say:
'We built our nest compact and warm,
But cruel boys came round our way
And took our summerhouse by storm.
'They crushed the eggs so neatly laid;
So now we sit with drooping wing,
And watch the ruin they have made,
Too late to build, too sad to sing.'

Heart's Chill Between

I did not chide him, though I knew
That he was false to me.
Chide the exhaling of the dew,
The ebbing of the sea,
The fading of a rosy hue,—
But not inconstancy.
Why strive for love when love is o'er?
Why bind a restive heart?—
He never knew the pain I bore
In saying: 'We must part;
Let us be friends and nothing more.'
—Oh, woman's shallow art!
But it is over, it is done,—
I hardly heed it now;
So many weary years have run
Since then, I think not how
Things might have been,—but greet each one
With an unruffled brow.
What time I am where others be,
My heart seems very calm—
Stone calm; but if all go from me,
There comes a vague alarm,
A shrinking in the memory
From some forgotten harm.
And often through the long, long night,
Waking when none are near,
I feel my heart beat fast with fright,
Yet know not what I fear.
Oh how I long to see the light,
And the sweet birds to hear!

To have the sun upon my face,
To look up through the trees,
To walk forth in the open space
And listen to the breeze,—

And not to dream the burial-place
Is clogging my weak knees.
Sometimes I can nor weep nor pray,
But am half stupefied:
And then all those who see me say
Mine eyes are opened wide
And that my wits seem gone away—
Ah, would that I had died!
Would I could die and be at peace,
Or living could forget!
My grief nor grows nor doth decrease,
But ever is:—and yet
Methinks, now, that all this shall cease
Before the sun shall set.

Heartsease In My Garden Bed

Heartsease in my garden bed,
With sweetwilliam white and red,
Honeysuckle on my wall: -
Heartsease blossoms in my heart
When sweet William comes to call,
But it withers when we part,
And the honey-trumpets fall.

Herself A Rose Who Bore The Rose

Herself a rose, who bore the Rose,
She bore the Rose and felt its thorn.
All loveliness new-born
Took on her bosom its repose,
And slept and woke there night and morn.
Lily herself, she bore the one
Fair Lily; sweeter, whiter, far
Than she or others are:
The Sun of Righteousness her Son,
She was His morning star.
She gracious, He essential Grace,
He was the Fountain, she the rill:
Her goodness to fulfil
And gladness, with proportioned pace
He led her steps through good and ill.
Christ's mirror she of grace and love,
Of beauty and of life and death:
By hope and love and faith
Transfigured to His likeness, 'Dove,
Spouse, Sister, Mother,' Jesus saith.

Holy Innocents

Sleep, little Baby, sleep,
The holy Angels love thee,
And guard thy bed, and keep
A blessed watch above thee.
No spirit can come near
Nor evil beast to harm thee:
Sleep, Sweet, devoid of fear
Where nothing need alarm thee.
The Love which doth not sleep,
The eternal arms around thee:
The shepherd of the sheep
In perfect love has found thee.
Sleep through the holy night,
Christ-kept from snare and sorrow,
Until thou wake to light
And love and warmth to-morrow.

Hope Is Like A Harebell Trembling From Its Birth

Hope is like a harebell trembling from its birth,
Love is like a rose the joy of all the earth;
Faith is like a lily lifted high and white,
Love is like a lovely rose the world's delight;
Harebells and sweet lilies show a thornless growth,
But the rose with all its thorns excels them both.

Hop-O'-My-Thumb And Little Jack Horner

Hop-o'-my-thumb and little Jack Horner,
What do you mean by tearing and fighting?
Sturdy dog Trot close round the corner,
I never caught him growling and biting.

Hopping Frog, Hop Here And Be Seen

Hopping frog, hop here and be seen,
I'll not pelt you with stick or stone:
Your cap is laced and your coat is green;
Good bye, we'll let each other alone.
Plodding toad, plod here and be looked at,
You the finger of scorn is crooked at:
But though you're lumpish, you're harmless too;
You won't hurt me, and I won't hurt you.

How Many Seconds In A Minute?

How many seconds in a minute?
Sixty, and no more in it.
How many minutes in an hour?
Sixty for sun and shower.
How many hours in a day?
Twenty-four for work and play.
How many days in a week?
Seven both to hear and speak.
How many weeks in a month?
Four, as the swift moon runneth.
How many months in a year?
Twelve the almanack makes clear.
How many years in an age?
One hundred says the sage.
How many ages in time?
No one knows the rhyme.

Hurt No Living Thing

Hurt no living thing:
Ladybird, nor butterfly,
Nor moth with dusty wing,
Nor cricket chirping cheerily,
Nor grasshopper so light of leap,
Nor dancing gnat, nor beetle fat,
Nor harmless worms that creep.

I Am A King

I am a King,
Or an Emperor rather,
I wear crown-imperial
And prince's-feather;
Golden-rod is the sceptre
I wield and wag,
And a broad purple flag-flower
Waves for my flag.
Elder the pithy
With old-man and sage,
These are my councillors
Green in old age;
Lord-and-ladies in silence
Stand round me and wait,
While gay ragged-robin
Makes bows at my gate.

I Caught A Little Ladybird

I caught a little ladybird
That flies far away;
I caught a little lady wife
That is both staid and gay.
Come back, my scarlet ladybird,
Back from far away;
I weary of my dolly wife,
My wife that cannot play.

I Dreamt I Caught A Little Owl

'I dreamt I caught a little owl
And the bird was blue -'
'But you may hunt for ever
And not find such a one.'
'I dreamt I set a sunflower,
And red as blood it grew -'
'But such a sunflower never
Bloomed beneath the sun.'

I Dug And Dug Amongst The Snow

I dug and dug amongst the snow,
And thought the flowers would never grow;
I dug and dug amongst the sand,
And still no green thing came to hand.
Melt, O snow! the warm winds blow
To thaw the flowers and melt the snow;
But all the winds from every land
Will rear no blossom from the sand.

I Have A Little Husband

I have a little husband
And he is gone to sea,
The winds that whistle round his ship
Fly home to me.
The winds that sigh about me
Return again to him;
So I would fly, if only I
Were light of limb.

I Have A Poll Parrot

I have a Poll parrot,
And Poll is my doll,
And my nurse is Polly,
And my sister Poll.
'Polly!' cried Polly,
'Don't tear Polly, dolly' -
While soft-hearted Poll
Trembled for the doll.

I Have But One Rose In The World

I have but one rose in the world,
And my one rose stands a-drooping:
Oh, when my single rose is dead
There'll be but thorns for stooping.

I Know A Baby, Such A Baby

I know a baby, such a baby, -
Round blue eyes and cheeks of pink,
Such an elbow furrowed with dimples,
Such a wrist where creases sink.
'Cuddle and love me, cuddle and love me,'
Crows the mouth of coral pink:
Oh, the bald head, and, oh, the sweet lips,
And, oh, the sleepy eyes that wink!

I Know You Not

O Christ, the Vine with living Fruit,
The twelvefold-fruited Tree of Life,
The Balm in Gilead after strife,
The valley Lily and the Rose;
Stronger than Lebanon, Thou Root;
Sweeter than clustered grapes, Thou Vine;
O Best, Thou Vineyard of red wine,
Keeping thy best wine till the close.
Pearl of great price Thyself alone,
And ruddier than the ruby Thou;
Most precious lightning Jasper stone,
Head of the corner spurned before:
Fair Gate of pearl, Thyself the Door;
Clear golden Street, Thyself the Way;
By Thee we journey toward Thee now,
Through Thee shall enter Heaven one day.
I thirst for Thee, full fount and flood;
My heart calls Thine, as deep to deep:
Dost Thou forget Thy sweat and pain,
They provocation on the Cross?
Heart-pierced for me, vouchsafe to keep
The purchase of Thy lavished Blood:
The gain is Thine, Lord, if I gain;
Or if I lose, Thine own the loss.
At midnight (saith the Parable)
A cry was made, the Bridegroom came;
Those who were ready entered in:
The rest, shut out in death and shame,
Strove all too late that Feast to win,
Their die was cast, and fixed their lot;

A gulf divided Heaven from Hell;
The Bridegroom said—I know you not.
But Who is this that shuts the door,
And saith—I know you not—to them?
I see the wounded hands and side,

The brow thorn-tortured long ago:
Yea; This Who grieved and bled and died,
This same is He Who must condemn;
He called, but they refused to know;
So now He hears their cry no more.

I loved you first: but afterwards your love

I loved you first: but afterwards your love,
Outsoaring mine, sang such a loftier song
As drowned the friendly cooings of my dove.
Which owes the other most? My love was long,
And yours one moment seemed to wax more strong;
I loved and guessed at you, you contrued me
And loved me for what might or might not be—
Nay, weights and measures do us both a wrong.
For verily love knows not 'mine' or 'thine';
With separate 'I' and 'thou' free love has done,
For one is both and both are one in love:
Rich love knows nought of 'thine that is not mine';
Both have the strength and both the length thereof,
Both of us, of the love which makes us one.

I Planted A Hand

I planted a hand
And there came up a palm,
I planted a heart
And there came up balm.
Then I planted a wish,
But there sprang a thorn,
While heaven frowned with thunder
And earth sighed forlorn.

If

If he would come to-day, to-day, to-day,
O, what a day to-day would be!
But now he's away, miles and miles away
From me across the sea.
O little bird, flying, flying, flying
To your nest in the warm west,
Tell him as you pass that I am dying,
As you pass home to your nest.
I have a sister, I have a brother,
A faithful hound, a tame white dove;
But I had another, once I had another,
And I miss him, my love, my love!
In this weary world it is so cold, so cold,
While I sit here all alone;
I would not like to wait and to grow old,
But just to be dead and gone.
Make me fair when I lie dead on my bed,
Fair where I am lying:
Perhaps he may come and look upon me dead—
He for whom I am dying.
Dig my grave for two, with a stone to show it,
And on the stone write my name;
If he never comes, I shall never know it,
But sleep on all the same.

If A Mouse Could Fly

If a mouse could fly,
Or if a crow could swim,
Or if a sprat could walk and talk,
I'd like to be like him.
If a mouse could fly,
He might fly away;
Or if a crow could swim,
It might turn him grey;
Or if a sprat could walk and talk,
What would he find to say?

If A Pig Wore A Wig

If a pig wore a wig,
What could we say?
Treat him as a gentleman,
And say 'Good day.'
If his tail chanced to fail,
What could we do? -
Send him to the tailoress
To get one new.

If All Were Rain And Never Sun

If all were rain and never sun,
No bow could span the hill;
If all were sun and never rain,
There'd be no rainbow still.

If Hope Grew On A Bush

If hope grew on a bush,
And joy grew on a tree,
What a nosegay for the plucking
There would be!
But oh! in windy autumn,
When frail flowers wither,
What should we do for hope and joy,
Fading together?

If I Were A Queen

If I were a Queen,
What would I do?
I'd make you King,
And I'd wait on you.
If I were a King,
What would I do?
I'd make you Queen,
For I'd marry you.

If Only

If I might only love my God and die!
But now He bids me love Him and live on,
Now when the bloom of all my life is gone,
The pleasant half of life has quite gone by.
My tree of hope is lopped that spread so high,
And I forget how summer glowed and shone,
While autumn grips me with its fingers wan
And frets me with its fitful windy sigh.
When autumn passes then must winter numb,
And winter may not pass a weary while,
But when it passes spring shall flower again;
And in that spring who weepeth now shall smile,
Yea, they shall wax who now are on the wane,
Yea, they shall sing for love when Christ shall come.

If Stars Dropped Out Of Heaven

If stars dropped out of heaven,
And if flowers took their place,
The sky would still look very fair,
And fair earth's face.
Winged angels might fly down to us
To pluck the stars,
Be we could only long for flowers
Beyond the cloudy bars.

If The Moon Came From Heaven

If the moon came from heaven,
Talking all the way,
What could she have to tell us,
And what could she say?
'I've seen a hundred pretty things,
And seen a hundred gay;
But only think: I peep by night
And do not peep by day!'

If The Sun Could Tell Us Half

If the sun could tell us half
That he hears and sees,
Sometimes he would make us laugh,
Sometimes make us cry:
Think of all the birds that make
Homes among the trees;
Think of cruel boys who take
Birds that cannot fly.

In An Artist's Studio

One face looks out from all his canvases,
One selfsame figure sits or walks or leans:
We found her hidden just behind those screens,
That mirror gave back all her loveliness.
A queen in opal or in ruby dress,
A nameless girl in freshest summer-greens,
A saint, an angel -- every canvas means
The same one meaning, neither more nor less.
He feeds upon her face by day and night,
And she with true kind eyes looks back on him,
Fair as the moon and joyful as the light:
Not wan with waiting, not with sorrow dim;
Not as she is, but was when hope shone bright;
Not as she is, but as she fills his dream.

In Progress

Ten years ago it seemed impossible
That she should ever grow so calm as this,
With self-remembrance in her warmest kiss
And dim dried eyes like an exhausted well.
Slow-speaking when she had some fact to tell,
Silent with long-unbroken silences,
Centered in self yet not unpleased to please,
Gravely monotonous like a passing bell.
Mindful of drudging daily common things,
Patient at pastime, patient at her work,
Wearied perhaps but strenuous certainly.
Sometimes I fancy we may one day see
Her head shoot forth seven stars from where they lurk
And her eyes lightnings and her shoulders wings.

In The Bleak Midwinter

In the bleak midwinter, frosty wind made moan,
Earth stood hard as iron, water like a stone;
Snow had fallen, snow on snow, snow on snow,
In the bleak midwinter, long ago.
Our God, Heaven cannot hold Him, nor earth sustain;
Heaven and earth shall flee away when He comes to reign.
In the bleak midwinter a stable place sufficed
The Lord God Almighty, Jesus Christ.
Enough for Him, Whom cherubim, worship night and day,
Breastful of milk, and a mangerful of hay;
Enough for Him, Whom angels fall before,
The ox and ass and camel which adore.
Angels and archangels may have gathered there,
Cherubim and seraphim thronged the air;
But His mother only, in her maiden bliss,
Worshipped the beloved with a kiss.
What can I give Him, poor as I am?
If I were a shepherd, I would bring a lamb;
If I were a Wise Man, I would do my part;
Yet what I can I give Him: give my heart.

In The Meadow - What In The Meadow?

In the meadow - what in the meadow?
Bluebells, buttercups, meadowsweet,
And fairy rings for the children's feet
In the meadow.
In the garden - what in the garden?
Jacob's-ladder and Solomon's-seal,
And Love-lies-bleeding beside All-heal
In the garden.

In The Round Tower At Jhansi

A hundred, a thousand to one; even so;
Not a hope in the world remained:
The swarming howling wretches below
Gained and gained and gained.
Skene looked at his pale young wife:—
'Is the time come?'—'The time is come!'—
Young, strong, and so full of life:
The agony struck them dumb.
Close his arm about her now,
Close her cheek to his,
Close the pistol to her brow—
God forgive them this!
'Will it hurt much?'—'No, mine own:
I wish I could bear the pang for both.'
'I wish I could bear the pang alone:
Courage, dear, I am not loth.'
Kiss and kiss: 'It is not pain
Thus to kiss and die.
One kiss more.'—'And yet one again.'—
'Good-bye.'—'Good-bye.'

In The Willow Shade

I sat beneath a willow tree,
Where water falls and calls;
While fancies upon fancies solaced me,
Some true, and some were false.
Who set their heart upon a hope
That never comes to pass,
Droop in the end like fading heliotrope
The sun's wan looking-glass.
Who set their will upon a whim
Clung to through good and ill,
Are wrecked alike whether they sink or swim,
Or hit or miss their will.
All things are vain that wax and wane,
For which we waste our breath;
Love only doth not wane and is not vain,
Love only outlives death.
A singing lark rose toward the sky,
Circling he sang amain;
He sang, a speck scarce visible sky-high,
And then he sank again.
A second like a sunlit spark
Flashed singing up his track;
But never overtook that foremost lark,
And songless fluttered back.
A hovering melody of birds
Haunted the air above;
They clearly sang contentment without words,
And youth and joy and love.
O silvery weeping willow tree
With all leaves shivering,

Have you no purpose but to shadow me
Beside this rippled spring?

On this first fleeting day of Spring,
For Winter is gone by,
And every bird on every quivering wing
Floats in a sunny sky;
On this first Summer-like soft day,
While sunshine steeps the air,
And every cloud has gat itself away,
And birds sing everywhere.
Have you no purpose in the world
But thus to shadow me
With all your tender drooping twigs unfurled,
O weeping willow tree?
With all your tremulous leaves outspread
Betwixt me and the sun,
While here I loiter on a mossy bed
With half my work undone;
My work undone, that should be done
At once with all my might;
For after the long day and lingering sun
Comes the unworking night.
This day is lapsing on its way,
Is lapsing out of sight;
And after all the chances of the day
Comes the resourceless night.
The weeping willow shook its head
And stretched its shadow long;
The west grew crimson, the sun smoldered red,
The birds forbore a song.
Slow wind sighed through the willow leaves,
The ripple made a moan,
The world drooped murmuring like a thing that grieves;
And then I felt alone.

I rose to go, and felt the chill,

And shivered as I went;
Yet shivering wondered, and I wonder still,
What more that willow meant;
That silvery weeping willow tree
With all leaves shivering,
Which spent one long day overshadowing me
Beside a spring in Spring.

Introspective

I wish it were over the terrible pain,
Pang after pang again and again;
First the shattering ruining blow,
Then the probing steady and slow.
Did I wince? I did not faint:
My soul broke but was not bent;
Up I stand like a blasted tree
By the shore of the shivering sea.
On my boughs neither leaf nor fruit,
No sap in my uttermost root,
Brooding in an anguish dumb
On the short past and the long to come.
Dumb I was when the ruin fell,
Dumb I remain and will never tell:
O my soul I talk with thee
But not another the sight must see.
I did not start when the torture stung,
I did not faint when the torture wrung;
Let it come tenfold if come it must
But I will not groan when I bite the dust.

Is It Well With The Child?

SAFE where I cannot die yet,
Safe where I hope to lie too,
Safe from the fume and the fret;
You, and you,
Whom I never forget.
Safe from the frost and the snow,
Safe from the storm and the sun,
Safe where the seeds wait to grow
One by one,
And to come back in blow.

Is The Moon Tired? She Looks So Pale

Is the moon tired? she looks so pale
Within her misty veil:
She scales the sky from east to west,
And takes no rest.
Before the coming of the night
The moon shows papery white;
Before the dawning of the day
She fades away.

January Cold Desolate

January cold desolate;
February all dripping wet;
March wind ranges;
April changes;
Birds sing in tune
To flowers of May,
And sunny June
Brings longest day;
In scorched July
The storm-clouds fly
Lightning-torn;
August bears corn,
September fruit;
In rough October
Earth must disrobe her;
Stars fall and shoot
In keen November;
And night is long
And cold is strong
In bleak December.

Jesus, Do I Love Thee?

Jesus, do I love Thee?
Thou art far above me,
Seated out of sight
Hid in Heavenly Light
Of most highest height.
Martyred hosts implore Thee,
Seraphs fall before Thee,
Angels and Archangels,
Cherub throngs adore Thee;
Blessed She that bore Thee!
All the Saints approve Thee,
All the Virgins love Thee.
I show as a blot
Blood hath cleansed not,
As a barren spot
In Thy fruitful lot.
I, fig-tree fruit-unbearing;
Thou, righteous Judge unsparing:
What canst Thou do more to me
That shall not more undo me?
Thy Justice hath a sound—
Why cumbereth it the ground?
Thy Love with stirrings stronger
Pleads—Give it one year longer.
Thou giv'st me time: but who
Save Thou shall give me dew;
Shall feed my root with Blood,
And stir my sap for good?
Oh, by Thy Gifts that shame me,
Give more lest they condemn me:

Good Lord, I ask much of Thee,
But most I ask to love Thee;
Kind Lord, be mindful of me,
Love me, and make me love Thee.

Kookoorookoo! Kookoorookoo!

'Kookoorookoo! kookoorookoo!'
Crows the cock before the morn;
'Kikirikee! kikirikee!'
Roses in the east are born.
'Kookoorookoo! kookoorookoo!'
Early birds begin their singing;
'Kikirikee! kikirikee!'
The day, the day, the day is springing.

L. E. L.

'Whose heart was breaking for a little love.'
Downstairs I laugh, I sport and jest with all;
But in my solitary room above
I turn my face in silence to the wall;
My heart is breaking for a little love.
Though winter frosts are done,
And birds pair every one,
And leaves peep out, for springtide is begun.
I feel no spring, while spring is wellnigh blown,
I find no nest, while nests are in the grove:
Woe's me for mine own heart that dwells alone,
My heart that breaketh for a little love.
While golden in the sun
Rivulets rise and run,
While lilies bud, for springtide is begun.
All love, are loved, save only I; their hearts
Beat warm with love and joy, beat full thereof:
They cannot guess, who play the pleasant parts,
My heart is breaking for a little love.
While beehives wake and whirr,
And rabbit thins his fur,
In living spring that sets the world astir.
I deck myself with skills and jewelry,
I plume myself like any mated dove:
They praise my rustling show, and never see
My heart is breaking for a little love.
While sprouts green lavender
With rosemary and myrrh,
For in quick spring the sap is all astir.
Perhaps some saints in glory guess the truth,

Perhaps some angels read it as they move,
And cry one to another full of ruth,
'Her heart is breaking for a little love.'
Though other things have birth,

And leap and sing for mirth,
When springtime wakes and clothes and feeds the earth.
Yet saith a saint: 'Take patience for thy scathe;'
Yet saith an angel: 'Wait, for thou shalt prove
True best is last, true life is born of death,
O thou, heart-broken for a little love.
Then love shall fill they girth,
And love make fat thy dearth,
When new spring builds new heaven and clean new earth.'

Lady Maggie

You must not call me Maggie, you must not call me Dear,
For I'm Lady of the Manor now stately to see;
And if there comes a babe, as there may some happy year,
'Twill be little lord or lady at my knee.
Oh, but what ails you, my sailor cousin Phil,
That you shake and turn white like a cockcrow ghost?
You're as white as I turned once down by the mill,
When one told me you and ship and crew were lost:
Philip my playfellow, when we were boy and girl
(It was the Miller's Nancy told it to me),
Philip with the merry life in lip and curl,
Philip my playfellow drowned in the sea!
I thought I should have fainted, but I did not faint;
I stood stunned at the moment, scarcely sad,
Till I raised my wail of desolate complaint
For you, my cousin, brother, all I had.
They said I looked so pale—some say so fair—
My lord stopped in passing to soothe me back to life:
I know I missed a ringlet from my hair
Next morning; and now I am his wife.
Look at my gown, Philip, and look at my ring,
I'm all crimson and gold from top to toe:
All day long I sit in the sun and sing,
Where in the sun red roses blush and blow.
And I'm the rose of roses says my lord;
And to him I'm more than the sun in the sky,
While I hold him fast with the golden cord
Of a curl, with the eyelash of an eye.
His mother said 'fie,' and his sisters cried 'shame,'
His highborn ladies cried 'shame' from their place:

They said 'fie' when they only heard my name,
But fell silent when they saw my face.

Am I so fair, Philip? Philip, did you think
I was so fair when we played boy and girl,
Where blue forget-me-nots bloomed on the brink
Of our stream which the mill-wheel sent a whirl?
If I was fair then sure I'm fairer now,
Sitting where a score of servants stand,
With a coronet on high days for my brow
And almost a sceptre for my hand.
You're but a sailor, Philip, weatherbeaten brown,
A stranger on land and at home on the sea,
Coasting as best you may from town to town:
Coasting along do you often think of me?
I'm a great lady in a sheltered bower,
With hands grown white through having nought to do:
Yet sometimes I think of you hour after hour
Till I nigh wish myself a child with you.

Last Night

Where were you last night? I watched at the gate;
I went down early, I stayed down late.
Were you snug at home, I should like to know,
Or were you in the coppice wheedling Kate?
She's a fine girl, with a fine clear skin;
Easy to woo, perhaps not hard to win.
Speak up like a man and tell me the truth:
I'm not one to grow downhearted and thin.
If you love her best speak up like a man;
It's not I will stand in the light of your plan:
Some girls might cry and scold you a bit,
And say they couldn't bear it; but I can.
Love was pleasant enough, and the days went fast;
Pleasant while it lasted, but it needn't last;
Awhile on the wax and awhile on the wane,
Now dropped away into the past.
Was it pleasant to you? To me it was;
Now clean gone as an image from glass,
As a goodly rainbow that fades away,
As dew that steams upward from the grass,
As the first spring day, or the last summer day,
As the sunset flush that leaves heaven grey,
As a flame burnt out for lack of oil,
Which no pains relight or ever may.
Good luck to Kate and good luck to you:
I guess she'll be kind when you come to woo.
I wish her a pretty face that will last,
I wish her a husband steady and true.
Hate you? not I, my very good friend;
All things begin and all have an end.

But let broken be broken; I put no faith
In quacks who set up to patch and mend.

Just my love and one word to Kate:
Not to let time slip if she means to mate;—
For even such a thing has been known
As to miss the chance while we weigh and wait.

Later Life

Something this foggy day, a something which
Is neither of this fog nor of today,
Has set me dreaming of the winds that play
Past certain cliffs, along one certain beach,
And turn the topmost edge of waves to spray:
Ah pleasant pebbly strand so far away,
So out of reach while quite within my reach,
As out of reach as India or Cathay!
I am sick of where I am and where I am not,
I am sick of foresight and of memory,
I am sick of all I have and all I see,
I am sick of self, and there is nothing new;
Oh weary impatient patience of my lot!
Thus with myself: how fares it, Friends, with you?

Let Me Go

When I come to the end of the road
And the sun has set for me
I want no rites in a gloom filled room
Why cry for a soul set free?
Miss me a little, but not for long
And not with your head bowed low
Remember the love that once we shared
Miss me, but let me go.
For this is a journey we all must take
And each must go alone.
It's all part of the master plan
A step on the road to home.
When you are lonely and sick at heart
Go the friends we know.
Laugh at all the things we used to do
Miss me, but let me go.
When I am dead my dearest
Sing no sad songs for me
Plant thou no roses at my head
Nor shady cypress tree
Be the green grass above me
With showers and dewdrops wet
And if thou wilt remember
And if thou wilt, forget.
I shall not see the shadows,
I shall not fear the rain;
I shall not hear the nightingale
Sing on as if in pain;
And dreaming through the twilight
That doth not rise nor set,

Haply I may remember,
And haply may forget.

Lie A-Bed

Lie a-bed,
Sleepy head,
Shut up eyes, bo-peep;
Till daybreak
Never wake: -
Baby, sleep.

Life And Death

Life is not sweet. One day it will be sweet
To shut our eyes and die:
Nor feel the wild flowers blow, nor birds dart by
With flitting butterfly,
Nor grass grow long above our heads and feet,
Nor hear the happy lark that soars sky high,
Nor sigh that spring is fleet and summer fleet,
Nor mark the waxing wheat,
Nor know who sits in our accustomed seat.
Life is not good. One day it will be good
To die, then live again;
To sleep meanwhile: so not to feel the wane
Of shrunk leaves dropping in the wood,
Nor hear the foamy lashing of the main,
Nor mark the blackened bean-fields, nor where stood
Rich ranks of golden grain
Only dead refuse stubble clothe the plain:
Asleep from risk, asleep from pain.

Light Love

'Oh, sad thy lot before I came,
But sadder when I go;
My presence but a flash of flame,
A transitory glow
Between two barren wastes like snow.
What wilt thou do when I am gone,
Where wilt thou rest, my dear?
For cold thy bed to rest upon,
And cold the falling year
Whose withered leaves are lost and sere.'
She hushed the baby at her breast,
She rocked it on her knee:
'And I will rest my lonely rest,
Warmed with the thought of thee,
Rest lulled to rest by memory.'
She hushed the baby with her kiss,
She hushed it with her breast:
'Is death so sadder much than this—
Sure death that builds a nest
For those who elsewhere cannot rest?'
'Oh, sad thy note, my mateless dove,
With tender nestling cold;
But hast thou ne'er another love
Left from the days of old,
To build thy nest of silk and gold,
To warm thy paleness to a blush
When I am far away—
To warm thy coldness to a flush,
And turn thee back to May,
And turn thy twilight back to day?'

She did not answer him again,
But leaned her face aside,
Weary with the pang of shame and pain,
And sore with wounded pride:
He knew his very soul had lied.
She strained his baby in her arms,

His baby to her heart:
'Even let it go, the love that harms:
We twain will never part;
Mine own, his own, how dear thou art.'
'Now never teaze me, tender-eyed,
Sigh-voiced,' he said in scorn:
'For nigh at hand there blooms a bride,
My bride before the morn;
Ripe-blooming she, as thou forlorn.
Ripe-blooming she, my rose, my peach;
She woos me day and night:
I watch her tremble in my reach;
She reddens, my delight,
She ripens, reddens in my sight.'
'And is she like a sunlit rose?
Am I like withered leaves?
Haste where thy spiced garden blows:
But in bare Autumn eves
Wilt thou have store of harvest sheaves?
Thou leavest love, true love behind,
To seek a love as true;
Go, seek in haste: but wilt thou find?
Change new again for new;
Pluck up, enjoy—yea, trample too.
'Alas for her, poor faded rose,
Alas for her her, like me,
Cast down and trampled in the snows.'
'Like thee? nay, not like thee:

She leans, but from a guarded tree.
Farewell, and dream as long ago,
Before we ever met:
Farewell; my swift-paced horse seems slow.'
She raised her eyes, not wet
But hard, to Heaven: 'Does God forget?'

Long Barren

Thou who didst hang upon a barren tree,
My God, for me;
Though I till now be barren, now at length
Lord, give me strength
To bring forth fruit to Thee.
Thou who didst bear for me the crown of thorn,
Spitting and scorn;
Though I till now have put forth thorns, yet now
Strengthen me Thou
That better fruit be borne.
Thou Rose of Sharon, Cedar of broad roots,
Vine of sweet fruits,
Thou Lily of the vale with fadeless leaf,
Of thousands Chief,
Feed Thou my feeble shoots.

Lord Jesus, Who Would Think That I Am Thine?

Lord Jesus, who would think that I am Thine?
Ah, who would think
Who sees me ready to turn back or sink,
That Thou art mine?
I cannot hold Thee fast though Thou art mine:
Hold Thou me fast,
So earth shall know at last and heaven at last
That I am Thine.

Love Came Down At Christmas

Love came down at Christmas,
Love all lovely, love divine;
Love was born at Christmas,
Star and angels gave the sign.
Worship we the Godhead,
Love incarnate, love divine;
Worship we our Jesus:
But wherewith for sacred sign?
Love shall be our token,
Love shall be yours and love be mine,
Love to God and to all men,
Love for plea and gift and sign.

Love From The North

I had a love in soft south land,
Beloved through April far in May;
He waited on my lightest breath,
And never dared to say me nay.
He saddened if my cheer was sad,
But gay he grew if I was gay;
We never differed on a hair,
My yes his yes, my nay his nay.
The wedding hour was come, the aisles
Were flushed with sun and flowers that day;
I pacing balanced in my thoughts:
'It's quite too late to think of nay.'—
My bridegroom answered in his turn,
Myself had almost answered 'yea:'
When through the flashing nave I heard
A struggle and resounding 'nay.'
Bridemaids and bridegroom shrank in fear,
But I stood high who stood at bay:
'And if I answer yea, fair Sir,
What man art thou to bar with nay?'
He was a strong man from the north,
Light-locked, with eyes of dangerous grey:
'Put yea by for another time
In which I will not say thee nay.'
He took me in his strong white arms,
He bore me on his horse away
O'er crag, morass, and hairbreadth pass,
But never asked me yea or nay.
He made me fast with book and bell,
With links of love he makes me stay;

Till now I've neither heart nor power
Nor will nor wish to say him nay.

Love Me - I Love You

Love me - I love you,
Love me, my baby;
Sing it high, sing it low,
Sing it as may be.
Mother's arms under you,
Her eyes above you;
Sing it high, sing it low,
Love me - I love you.

Lullaby, Oh, Lullaby!

Lullaby, oh, lullaby!
Flowers are closed and lambs are sleeping;
Lullaby, oh, lullaby!
Stars are up, the moon is peeping;
Lullaby, oh, lullaby!
While the birds are silence keeping,
(Lullaby, oh, lullaby!)
Sleep, my baby, fall a-sleeping,
Lullaby, oh, lullaby!

Maiden May

Maiden May sat in her bower,
In her blush rose bower in flower,
Sweet of scent;
Sat and dreamed away an hour,
Half content, half uncontent.
'Why should rose blossoms be born,
Tender blossoms, on a thorn
Though so sweet?
Never a thorn besets the corn
Scentless in its strength complete.
'Why are roses all so frail,
At the mercy of a gale,
Of a breath?
Yet so sweet and perfect pale,
Still so sweet in life and death.'
Maiden May sat in her bower,
In her blush rose bower in flower,
Where a linnet
Made one bristling branch the tower
For her nest and young ones in it.
'Gay and clear the linnet trills;
Yet the skylark only, thrills
Heaven and earth
When he breasts the height, and fills
Height and depth with song and mirth.
'Nightingales which yield to night
Solitary strange delight,
Reign alone:
But the lark for all his height
Fills no solitary throne;

'While he sings, a hundred sing;
Wing their flight below his wing
Yet in flight;
Each a lovely joyful thing
To the measure of its delight.
'Why then should a lark be reckoned
One alone, without a second
Near his throne?
He in skyward flight unslackened,
In his music, not alone.'
Maiden May sat in her bower;
Her own face was like a flower
Of the prime,
Half in sunshine, half in shower,
In the year's most tender time.
Her own thoughts in silent song
Musically flowed along,
Wise, unwise,
Wistful, wondering, weak or strong:
As brook shallows sink or rise.
Other thoughts another day,
Maiden May, will surge and sway
Round your heart;
Wake, and plead, and turn at bay,
Wisdom part, and folly part.
Time not far remote will borrow
Other joys, another sorrow,
All for you;
Not to-day, and yet to-morrow
Reasoning false and reasoning true.

Wherefore greatest? Wherefore least?
Hearts that starve and hearts that feast?
You and I?
Stammering Oracles have ceased,

And the whole earth stands at 'why?'
Underneath all things that be
Lies an unsolved mystery;
Over all
Spreads a veil impenetrably,
Spreads a dense unlifted pall.
Mystery of mysteries:
This creation hears and sees
High and low -
Vanity of vanities:
This we test and this we know.
Maiden May, the days of flowering
Nurse you now in sweet embowering,
Sunny days;
Bright with rainbows all the showering,
Bright with blossoms all the ways.
Close the inlet of your bower,
Close it close with thorn and flower,
Maiden May;
Lengthen out the shortening hour, -
Morrows are not as to-day.
Stay to-day which wanes too soon,
Stay the sun and stay the moon,
Stay your youth;
Bask you in the actual noon,
Rest you in the present truth.

Let to-day suffice to-day:
For itself to-morrow may
Fetch its loss,
Aim and stumble, say its say,
Watch and pray and bear its cross.

Maiden-Song

Long ago and long ago,
And long ago still,
There dwelt three merry maidens
Upon a distant hill.
One was tall Megan,
And one was dainty May,
But one was fair Margaret,
More fair than I can say,
Long ago and long ago.
When Megan plucked the thorny rose,
And when May pulled the brier,
Half the birds would swoop to see,
Half the beasts draw nigher;
Half the fishes of the streams
Would dart up to admire:
But when Margaret plucked a flag-flower,
Or poppy hot aflame,
All the beasts and all the birds
And all the fishes came
To her hand more soft than snow.
Strawberry leaves and May-dew
In brisk morning air,
Strawberry leaves and May-dew
Make maidens fair.
'I go for strawberry leaves,'
Megan said one day:
'Fair Margaret can bide at home,
But you come with me, May;
Up the hill and down the hill,
Along the winding way
You and I are used to go.'

So these two fair sisters
Went with innocent will
Up the hill and down again,
And round the homestead hill:
While the fairest sat at home,

Margaret like a queen,
Like a blush-rose, like the moon
In her heavenly sheen,
Fragrant-breathed as milky cow
Or field of blossoming bean,
Graceful as an ivy bough
Born to cling and lean;
Thus she sat to sing and sew.
When she raised her lustrous eyes
A beast peeped at the door;
When she downward cast her eyes
A fish gasped on the floor;
When she turned away her eyes
A bird perched on the sill,
Warbling out its heart of love,
Warbling warbling still,
With pathetic pleadings low.
Light-foot May with Megan
Sought the choicest spot,
Clothed with thyme-alternate grass:
Then, while day waxed hot,
Sat at ease to play and rest,
A gracious rest and play;
The loveliest maidens near or far,
When Margaret was away,
Who sat at home to sing and sew.
Sun-glow flushed their comely cheeks,
Wind-play tossed their hair,
Creeping things among the grass

Stroked them here and there;
Megan piped a merry note,
A fitful wayward lay,
While shrill as bird on topmost twig
Piped merry May;
Honey-smooth the double flow.
Sped a herdsman from the vale,
Mounting like a flame,
All on fire to hear and see,

With floating locks he came.
Looked neither north nor south,
Neither east nor west,
But sat him down at Megan's feet
As love-bird on his nest,
And wooed her with a silent awe,
With trouble not expressed;
She sang the tears into his eyes,
The heart out of his breast:
So he loved her, listening so.
She sang the heart out of his breast,
The words out of his tongue;
Hand and foot and pulse he paused
Till her song was sung.
Then he spoke up from his place
Simple words and true:
'Scanty goods have I to give,
Scanty skill to woo;
But I have a will to work,
And a heart for you:
Bid me stay or bid me go.'
Then Megan mused within herself:
'Better be first with him,
Than dwell where fairer Margaret sits,
Who shines my brightness dim,

For ever second where she sits,
However fair I be:
I will be lady of his love,
And he shall worship me;
I will be lady of his herds
And stoop to his degree,
At home where kids and fatlings grow.'
Sped a shepherd from the height
Headlong down to look,
(White lambs followed, lured by love
Of their shepherd's crook):
He turned neither east nor west,
Neither north nor south,

But knelt right down to May, for love
Of her sweet-singing mouth;
Forgot his flocks, his panting flocks
In parching hill-side drouth;
Forgot himself for weal or woe.
Trilled her song and swelled her song
With maiden coy caprice
In a labyrinth of throbs,
Pauses, cadences;
Clear-noted as a dropping brook,
Soft-noted like the bees,
Wild-noted as the shivering wind
Forlorn through forest trees:
Love-noted like the wood-pigeon
Who hides herself for love,
Yet cannot keep her secret safe,
But coos and coos thereof:
Thus the notes rang loud or low.
He hung breathless on her breath;
Speechless, who listened well;
Could not speak or think or wish

Till silence broke the spell.
Then he spoke, and spread his hands,
Pointing here and there:
'See my sheep and see the lambs,
Twin lambs which they bare.
All myself I offer you,
All my flocks and care,
Your sweet song hath moved me so.'
In her fluttered heart young May
Mused a dubious while:
'If he loves me as he says'--
Her lips curved with a smile:
'Where Margaret shines like the sun
I shine but like a moon;
If sister Megan makes her choice
I can make mine as soon;
At cockcrow we were sister-maids,
We may be brides at noon.'

Said Megan, 'Yes;' May said not 'No.'
Fair Margaret stayed alone at home,
Awhile she sang her song,
Awhile sat silent, then she thought:
'My sisters loiter long.'
That sultry noon had waned away,
Shadows had waxen great:
'Surely,' she thought within herself,
'My sisters loiter late.'
She rose, and peered out at the door,
With patient heart to wait,
And heard a distant nightingale
Complaining of its mate;
Then down the garden slope she walked,
Down to the garden gate,
Leaned on the rail and waited so.

The slope was lightened by her eyes
Like summer lightning fair,
Like rising of the haloed moon
Lightened her glimmering hair,
While her face lightened like the sun
Whose dawn is rosy white.
Thus crowned with maiden majesty
She peered into the night,
Looked up the hill and down the hill,
To left hand and to right,
Flashing like fire-flies to and fro.
Waiting thus in weariness
She marked the nightingale
Telling, if any one would heed,
Its old complaining tale.
Then lifted she her voice and sang,
Answering the bird:
Then lifted she her voice and sang,
Such notes were never heard
From any bird when Spring's in blow.
The king of all that country
Coursing far, coursing near,

Curbed his amber-bitted steed,
Coursed amain to hear;
All his princes in his train,
Squire, and knight, and peer,
With his crown upon his head,
His sceptre in his hand,
Down he fell at Margaret's knees
Lord king of all that land,
To her highness bending low.
Every beast and bird and fish
Came mustering to the sound,
Every man and every maid

From miles of country round:
Megan on her herdsman's arm,
With her shepherd May,
Flocks and herds trooped at their heels
Along the hill-side way;
No foot too feeble for the ascent,
Not any head too grey;
Some were swift and none were slow.
So Margaret sang her sisters home
In their marriage mirth;
Sang free birds out of the sky,
Beasts along the earth,
Sang up fishes of the deep--
All breathing things that move
Sang from far and sang from near
To her lovely love;
Sang together friend and foe;
Sang a golden-bearded king
Straightway to her feet,
Sang him silent where he knelt
In eager anguish sweet.
But when the clear voice died away,
When longest echoes died,
He stood up like a royal man
And claimed her for his bride.
So three maids were wooed and won
In a brief May-tide,

Long ago and long ago.

Margaret Has A Milking-Pail

Margaret has a milking-pail,
And she rises early;
Thomas has a threshing-flail,
And he's up betimes.
Sometimes crossing through the grass
Where the dew lies pearly,
They say 'Good morrow' as they pass
By the leafy limes.

Marvel Of Marvels

MARVEL of marvels, if I myself shall behold
With mine own eyes my King in His city of gold;
Where the least of lambs is spotless white in the fold,
Where the least and last of saints in spotless white is stoled,
Where the dimmest head beyond a moon is aureoled.
O saints, my beloved, now mouldering to mould in the mould,
Shall I see you lift your heads, see your cerements unroll'd,
See with these very eyes? who now in darkness and cold
Tremble for the midnight cry, the rapture, the tale untold,--
The Bridegroom cometh, cometh, His Bride to enfold!
Cold it is, my beloved, since your funeral bell was toll'd:
Cold it is, O my King, how cold alone on the wold!

Maude Clare

Out of the church she followed them
With a lofty step and mien:
His bride was like a village maid,
Maude Clare was like a queen.
"Son Thomas, " his lady mother said,
With smiles, almost with tears:
"May Nell and you but live as true
As we have done for years;
"Your father thirty years ago
Had just your tale to tell;
But he was not so pale as you,
Nor I so pale as Nell."
My lord was pale with inward strife,
And Nell was pale with pride;
My lord gazed long on pale Maude Clare
Or ever he kissed the bride.
"Lo, I have brought my gift, my lord,
Have brought my gift, " she said:
To bless the hearth, to bless the board,
To bless the marriage-bed.
"Here's my half of the golden chain
You wore about your neck,
That day we waded ankle-deep
For lilies in the beck:
"Here's my half of the faded leaves
We plucked from the budding bough,
With feet amongst the lily leaves, -
The lilies are budding now."
He strove to match her scorn with scorn,
He faltered in his place:

"Lady, " he said, - "Maude Clare, " he said, -
"Maude Clare, " – and hid his face.

She turn'd to Nell: "My Lady Nell,
I have a gift for you;
Though, were it fruit, the blooms were gone,
Or, were it flowers, the dew.
"Take my share of a fickle heart,
Mine of a paltry love:
Take it or leave it as you will,
I wash my hands thereof."
"And what you leave, " said Nell, "I'll take,
And what you spurn, I'll wear;
For he's my lord for better and worse,
And him I love Maude Clare.
"Yea, though you're taller by the head,
More wise and much more fair:
I'll love him till he loves me best,
Me best of all Maude Clare.

May

I cannot tell you how it was,
But this I know: it came to pass
Upon a bright and sunny day
When May was young; ah, pleasant May!
As yet the poppies were not born
Between the blades of tender corn;
The last egg had not hatched as yet,
Nor any bird foregone its mate.
I cannot tell you what it was,
But this I know: it did but pass.
It passed away with sunny May,
Like all sweet things it passed away,
And left me old, and cold, and gray.

Memory

I

I nursed it in my bosom while it lived,
I hid it in my heart when it was dead;
In joy I sat alone, even so I grieved
Alone and nothing said.
I shut the door to face the naked truth,
I stood alone—I faced the truth alone,
Stripped bare of self-regard or forms or ruth
Till first and last were shown.
I took the perfect balances and weighed;
No shaking of my hand disturbed the poise;
Weighed, found it wanting: not a word I said,
But silent made my choice.
None know the choice I made; I make it still.
None know the choice I made and broke my heart,
Breaking mine idol: I have braced my will
Once, chosen for once my part.
I broke it at a blow, I laid it cold,
Crushed in my deep heart where it used to live.
My heart dies inch by inch; the time grows old,
Grows old in which I grieve.

II

I have a room whereinto no one enters
Save I myself alone:
There sits a blessed memory on a throne,
There my life centres.
While winter comes and goes—oh tedious comer!
And while its nip-wind blows;
While bloom the bloodless lily and warm rose
Of lavish summer.

If any should force entrance he might see there
One buried yet not dead,
Before whose face I no more bow my head
Or bend my knee there;
But often in my worn life's autumn weather
I watch there with clear eyes,
And think how it will be in Paradise
When we're together.

Minnie And Mattie

Minnie and Mattie
And fat little May,
Out in the country,
Spending a day.
Such a bright day,
With the sun glowing,
And the trees half in leaf,
And the grass growing.
Pinky white pigling
Squeals through his snout,
Woolly white lambkin
Frisks all about.
Cluck! cluck! the nursing hen
Summons her folk, -
Ducklings all downy soft
Yellow as yolk.
Cluck! cluck! the mother hen
Summons her chickens
To peck the dainty bits
Found in her pickings.
Minnie and Mattie
And May carry posies,
Half of sweet violets,
Half of primroses.
Give the sun time enough,
Glowing and glowing,
He'll rouse the roses
And bring them blowing.
Don't wait for roses
Losing to-day,

O Minnie, Mattie,
And wise little May.
Violets and primroses
Blossom to-day
For Minnie and Mattie
And fat little May.

Minnie Bakes Oaten Cakes

Minnie bakes oaten cakes,
Minnie brews ale,
All because her Johnny's coming
Home from sea.
And she glows like a rose
Who was so pale,
And 'Are you sure the church clock goes?'
Says she.

www.ingramcontent.com/pod-product-compliance
Lightning Source LLC
LaVergne TN
LVHW091257150826
845673LV00006B/1450

9789394109711